# CAMBRIDGE LIBRARY COLLECTION

*Books of enduring scholarly value*

## Archaeology

The discovery of material remains from the recent or the ancient past has
always been a source of fascination, but the development of archaeology as
an academic discipline which interpreted such finds is relatively recent. It
was the work of Winckelmann at Pompeii in the 1760s which first revealed
the potential of systematic excavation to scholars and the wider public.
Pioneering figures of the nineteenth century such as Schliemann, Layard
and Petrie transformed archaeology from a search for ancient artifacts, by
means as crude as using gunpowder to break into a tomb, to a science which
drew from a wide range of disciplines - ancient languages and literature,
geology, chemistry, social history - to increase our understanding of human
life and society in the remote past.

## Ionia and the East

The archaeologist D. G. Hogarth (1862–1927) was, when he died, keeper of
the Ashmolean Museum and president of the Royal Geographical Society.
During his career he excavated in Cyprus, Egypt, Greece and Asia Minor.
His books about his travels and excavations were well received and *A
Wandering Scholar in the Levant* of 1896 (also reissued in this series) was
described by T. E. Lawrence as 'one of the best travel books ever written'.
This work, first published in 1909, contains six lectures on the origins of
Ionia. Hogarth presents and evaluates the theories of the origins of Ionian
culture that were popular at the time, and in the course of his discussion
he delivers the results of some of his own excavations, including those at
Ephesus in 1904. The work remains of interest to scholars and students of
the region and of the history of archaeology.

T0345435

Cambridge University Press has long been a pioneer in the reissuing of out-of-print titles from its own backlist, producing digital reprints of books that are still sought after by scholars and students but could not be reprinted economically using traditional technology. The Cambridge Library Collection extends this activity to a wider range of books which are still of importance to researchers and professionals, either for the source material they contain, or as landmarks in the history of their academic discipline.

Drawing from the world-renowned collections in the Cambridge University Library, and guided by the advice of experts in each subject area, Cambridge University Press is using state-of-the-art scanning machines in its own Printing House to capture the content of each book selected for inclusion. The files are processed to give a consistently clear, crisp image, and the books finished to the high quality standard for which the Press is recognised around the world. The latest print-on-demand technology ensures that the books will remain available indefinitely, and that orders for single or multiple copies can quickly be supplied.

The Cambridge Library Collection brings back to life books of enduring scholarly value (including out-of-copyright works originally issued by other publishers) across a wide range of disciplines in the humanities and social sciences and in science and technology.

# Ionia and the East

*Six Lectures Delivered Before
the University of London*

D. G. HOGARTH

CAMBRIDGE UNIVERSITY PRESS

Cambridge, New York, Melbourne, Madrid, Cape Town,
Singapore, São Paolo, Delhi, Tokyo, Mexico City

Published in the United States of America by Cambridge University Press, New York

www.cambridge.org
Information on this title: www.cambridge.org/9781108041942

© in this compilation Cambridge University Press 2012

This edition first published 1909
This digitally printed version 2012

ISBN 978-1-108-04194-2 Paperback

# IONIA AND THE EAST

HENRY FROWDE, M.A.
PUBLISHER TO THE UNIVERSITY OF OXFORD
LONDON, EDINBURGH, NEW YORK
TORONTO AND MELBOURNE

# IONIA AND THE EAST

## SIX LECTURES DELIVERED BEFORE
## THE UNIVERSITY OF LONDON

BY

### DAVID G. HOGARTH

FELLOW OF MAGDALEN COLLEGE; FELLOW OF THE BRITISH ACADEMY

WITH A MAP

OXFORD

AT THE CLARENDON PRESS

1909

OXFORD
PRINTED AT THE CLARENDON PRESS
BY HORACE HART, M.A.
PRINTER TO THE UNIVERSITY

# CONTENTS

# LECTURE I

## INTRODUCTION TO THE PROBLEM

THE purpose of these lectures is generally to consider the circumstances under which Hellenic civilization, properly so called, came into being, and in particular, the origin of that brilliant Ionian society which a French writer has named *le printemps de la Grèce*. Some fresh light and, it must be admitted, not a little fresh darkness have been shed upon the matter by recent archaeological discoveries. Some of these I can describe at first hand : others I am in some position to appreciate from having borne a part in similar research, and having gained experience during the last twenty years of wellnigh all the eastern Mediterranean lands whose divers civilizations had relat ons with the Ionian.

On the great interest of this question of Ionian origins to all students of antiquity, nay, to all students of civilization, I need not waste many words. Even in the face of recent discoveries at Sparta, it may be said without hesitation that the Greeks of western Asia Minor produced the first full bloom of what we call pure Hellenism, that is, a Greek civilization come to full consciousness of itself, and destined to attain the highest possibilities of the Hellenic genius. Whatever its claim to absolute priority in culture, however, the Ionian section of the Hellenic race, from the accident of geographical position, served more than any other for a vital link between East and West, and imposed its individual name on Oriental terminology as the designation of the whole Greek people. All who follow the development of free social institutions must regard with peculiar interest the land where the City State of Hellenic type first grew to adolescence. Students not only of literature, but of all the means of communication between man and man, know that it was in Ionia that the alphabet took the final shape in which the Greeks were to carry it about the civilized world. And who, that belongs to, or cares for, the republic of art, would ignore that ' bel élan de génie duquel est née la statuaire attique ' ?

Two theories have been propounded to account for the sudden appearance of a very high civilization in Ionia at the opening of the historic age. They are not necessarily mutually exclusive, and neither is necessarily false. But both were advanced rather as hypotheses to explain subsequent historic phenomena than as deductions from prehistoric evidence ; and though both have found large acceptance, the statement of them has always been vague. The first was that associated with the name of Ernst Curtius, who postulated the existence of a prehistoric Indo-European population in western Anatolia. This he held to be not aboriginal, but an earlier migratory wave of the same great stock which was to throw off the European Hellenes. The proto-Ionians, as he called them, who had branched off and entered Asia Minor by way of the north-western corner, had already established there a culture of Hellenic type ere the historic Ionian Migration from mainland Greece reached Asia. It was out of the amalgamation of this culture of theirs with that of their kindred, who subsequently joined them, stimulated further by Mesopotamian influences, that the historic Ionian civilization sprang with amazing rapidity to full growth. This theory, at the time it was propounded, was probable enough, but incapable of proof. Practically nothing could be adduced to illustrate the supposed culture of either of those Indo-European stocks before their fusion. From the little known of the Lydian language, from the Greek tradition of the origin of the Phrygians, from probable inference as to the racial character of certain pre-Ionian racial elements in Ionia, for example, the Lelegian and the Carian, Curtius could claim some justification for his pre-Ionian Indo-European in Asia Minor. But all further deduction remained ' in the air '.

The second theory was the outcome of the subsequent

revelation of prehistoric Aegean civilization.  It has taken
the form of a general asseveration that Ionian civilization
was essentially a survival of the Aegean, a *Nachleben mykeni-
scher Cultur.*  There were, however, no documents of early
Ionian culture sufficient to prove or disprove this view,
which was, perhaps, in the main an inference from Homer.
The Epos, supposed by many to have taken shape at Ionian
courts, was argued to reflect a sub-Mycenaean civilization.
Ergo, there was such a civilization in Ionia.

This theory, as I have said, is not necessarily exclusive
of the first.  It might, on the contrary, be held comple-
mentary and explanatory, determining the nature of the
original culture shared by the two contributory kindred
stocks of Curtius's creed.  But so far as I know, no one
who propounded the theory, ever explained precisely
whether it was both, or only one of those stocks, which
had formerly shared the full Aegean civilization ; whether
this civilization had been domiciled of old on the west
Anatolian coast, or only been introduced by the Ionian
Migration ; or whether the proto-Ionian shared it at all.
Those who held the view, most recently expounded in sub-
stance by Professor Ridgeway, that the Lelegian stock of
western Asia Minor was of close kin to the European
Pelasgic, and that the latter was the author of things
Mycenaean, inclined to regard Aegean culture as having been
shared from an early period by the Anatolian coastlands.
But they could not adduce sufficient archaeological evidence
to raise their theory out of the region of hypothesis.  Except
at Hissarlik in the extreme north-west and at one or two
points on Carian and Rhodian territory in the extreme
south, the eastern shore of the Aegean had yielded nothing
whatever pertaining to Aegean culture.

The adherents of both theories held also, in somewhat
indefinite language, that much of the impulse to develop
a culture higher than that prevailing previously either in
the region from which the colonists had come, or among
the littoral peoples of Asia Minor itself, resulted from
Ionian contact with certain older civilizations of the East,

notably the Mesopotamian. With this last region, however, the early Ionians, it was thought, had no direct communication, but only secondary relations through intermediary societies. These communicated Eastern influences both by land and by sea, and among them the Syro-Cappadocian or 'Hittite' society radiating its influence through Phrygia and Lydia, and the Phoenician, which had been pushing its trade in a westerly direction during the post-Aegean Dark Age, were the chief. Thanks to such relations, the Ionians received the model of commercial society and certain things indispensable to its progress, notably alphabetic writing and a coined medium of exchange, and at the same time became cognizant of processes of manufacture and art already well developed elsewhere. Thus encouraged, the natural genius of the Ionian race developed with remarkable rapidity. It soon outgrew its instructors and became, to some extent, their teacher, partly through a further colonial effort by which Ionia planted Ionians far outside the cradle of their original civilization. In particular it reacted on the land from which the first colonists had come, the easternmost part of the Greek peninsula, and was largely responsible for the rise of Attic culture.

What was held thus about the origin of Ionian civilization was held also in some degree about the origin of all that earliest civilization in Asia Minor, which the later Greeks ascribed to colonization from Europe, but differentiated as Dorian or Aeolic. But it was believed that the Ionian settlers had had the fortune to fall among a race more nearly kin to the Hellenic than were the Carian tribes of the south-western littoral, or the Mysians of the north. Hence the Ionian development proved the more peaceful and rapid, and attained to a higher plane of culture.

This is, I think, a fair summary of the most generally received opinion based on the researches and arguments of many authorities who wrote in the latter half of the last century. Opinion, and nothing more, however, it had to remain. The origin of any particular ancient culture is

necessarily an archæological question.  Some other culture,
contemporary with its beginnings, may have already developed a literature, and this may chance to make allusion
to it.  But such allusion can hardly be expected to throw
any but dim and uncertain light, since, *ex hypothesi*, we are
inquiring about a remote age, prior to the development of
lively human curiosity about alien peoples.  In this particular case, as it happens, the origin of what was actually
the earliest civilization, which developed any extant literature inspired by such curiosity, is under discussion.  Literary
evidence concerning the origin of Ionian civilization is to
be derived from authorities of which the earliest were
necessarily posterior by some centuries.  Their references
are seldom to be understood, and never safely to be applied,
without the help of archaeology.  Such are the Greek records
of local tradition, Greek archaeological statements of long
bygone fact, and Greek archaeological ratiocination, expressed by writers earlier than the establishment of any
objective standards for appraising archaeological evidence.
As examples of such literature, bearing conscious and
unconscious reference to the early story of Hellenic civilization, we have, on the one hand, the body of lays, which form
the basis, at any rate, of the Homeric *Iliad* and of most of
the Cyclic fragments which have survived ; and, on the other,
an historical work, written by an Asiatic Greek of great
perspicacity and learning not much more than half-way
through the first millennium B.C.  Herodotus recorded not
only much antecedent fact, but also local traditions of his day
in regard to this very matter.  To these authorities I shall
often refer later, and I only pause at this stage to enforce
my point about the comparative difficulty of understanding
and the danger of applying the evidence of early literature
to such a question as the origin of a civilization without
invoking the help of archaeological evidence, by reminding
you of two facts.  Firstly, the most close study of the
Homeric Epos in no way enabled scholars to assign to the
culture, there reflected, its just relative position in the
development of Aegean man, but, on the contrary, caused

a settled predisposition to mistake the times and places of his highest development. Secondly, Herodotus alone among extant Greek authors made any certain allusion to that remarkable early society of eastern Asia Minor, the Syro-Cappadocian or Hatti ; but his allusion excited little or no curiosity, and the society in question was not held of any account whatever, until hardly a generation ago. In fact, the measure of its necessary relation to the origins of that very Greek civilization, about which the Halicarnassian showed himself so curious, has yet to be appraised.

On archaeology, therefore, fell, and falls, the burden of proof in this inquiry. But archaeology, whatever its competence nowadays, was certainly in a very poor position to offer evidence up to the end of the nineteenth century. In the first place, it should have been able to take cognizance of a large and various body of material documents, illustrative not only of Ionian culture itself in its earliest stages, but also of the precedent condition in which the aboriginal populations of western Asia Minor and the future settlers from Europe were for some time before the latter passed across the Aegean Sea. In the second place, if it could claim adequate knowledge of the greater Eastern societies, by which Ionian culture was supposed to have been stimulated, it needed to have equal knowledge of the intermediary societies occupying the routes, whether by land or sea, over which the Mesopotamian and Nilotic influences had to travel westwards. What, however, was the case ? Without necessarily implying that it is in many respects different now, let me state it briefly as it stood at the close of the nineteenth century.

As regards Ionia itself, the tale of local documents relating to early stages of its cultural development was miserably short. Excavators have spent as much time and money on sites of west Asia Minor during the past generation as on any others round the Mediterranean. Prior to 1900 the exploration of Pergamum had been prosecuted on a large scale for nearly a quarter of a century. Before that the British excavations at Halicarnassus and Cnidus began and the superficial examinations of certain sites in the lower valley of the Maeander had been concluded. Ephesus, both town and temple, had been searched by Wood and abandoned ; but the town had already been reopened and been in process of re-examination for some years by the Austrian Archaeological Institute. Magnesia-on-Maeander was considered to have yielded up its secrets and all spoils, worth removal, to Humann and his colleagues. Priene had been finished by Wiegand and Miletus begun.

But of all these explorations—several of them most considerable enterprises—one thing can be said alike. They never served to expose any stratum of remains which could be referred to the early morning, still less to the dawn, of Hellenic civilization in western Asia. The nearest approaches to primitive strata were made by British explorers. At Branchidae Newton had the fortune to find certain relics of Ionian art of the seventh and sixth centuries on the surface of the soil, and at Ephesus Wood penetrated downwards to the remains of the Artemisium of the latter century, but there stopped short. Almost all the other great excavations were conducted without apparent intention to explore early strata. At Pergamum, Magnesia, and Priene the object of the explorers was to recover Hellenistic and Graeco-Roman evidence, mainly of an architectural nature, and the sites chosen were not such as offered good hope of anything of earlier date. The Roman city of Ephesus must have been built at one point or another over strata resultant from inhabitation since the earliest Ionian days ; but, during ten years of excavation, the Austrian explorers of the city have not touched those strata, and have been content to lay bare pavements and structures of Imperial times.

There is one notable exception, however, to be taken to this rule, that excavations conducted on any considerable scale in Hellenic Asia had so far not been directed to the earlier strata : that is, of course, the exploration of Hissarlik by Schliemann and Dörpfeld. Here you do not need to be reminded that an early site was probed to the bottom, and that successive layers were examined, which contained documents going far behind the earliest stage of Hellenic culture in Asia Minor. Apart, however, from the general prejudice, which long prevailed, against recognizing a causative relation between the prehistoric and the historic cultures of the Hellenic area, the particular circumstances of Hissarlik served to make scholars slow to admit a connexion between its remains and the Ionian question. The site lies comparatively remote from that part of the Anatolian coast where the higher Hellenic culture first developed. The remains of the earlier, and by far the most considerable, periods at Hissarlik attach themselves to a class distinct in certain respects from the general culture of prehistoric Greece, and not observed at all in Ionia. The remains, which were actually referred to the opening of the historic period, were scanty and illustrative of local decadence ; while others, which might also have been so referred, were confused with strata of earlier periods, and their significance was mistaken. The upshot was that from first to last the exploration of Hissarlik failed materially to affect the discussion of the Ionian problem.

For the earliest material documents of Ionian history, therefore, scholars had to look in the main to a small number of comparatively late Ionian architectural and sculptura remains, of which very few had been found in Ionia itself, and the exiguous majority came from Carian territory or Aegean isles, notably Delos ; to coins, of which the earliest were not dated before the seventh century ; and to a very few archaic inscriptions, whereof the very earliest again were not ascribed to quite so early a period. There had, indeed, been discovered a few local relics of human handiwork which were acknowledged to be more ancient. Such were the famous ' Sesostris ' figures on the cliffs of the Kara Bel near Nymphi ; the ' Niobe ' and some other primitive remains in Mount Sipylus ; and also the ruined ' Tantalus Tomb ' of Aeolic Smyrna and certain traces of a neighbouring settlement, and of shrines, forts, and look-out places in the hills behind. But the ' Sesostris ' figures and the ' Niobe ' were put out of court as Syro-Cappadocian memorials of a foreign and brief invasion from far inland ; and the scanty ' Tantalus ' remains had to bear witness alone in Ionia to proto-Ionian civilization.

If one turned to the lands marching with Ionia on the continental side, the case of archaeology appeared little better.  Lydia was (and for that matter still is) the least productive district of Asia Minor from an archaeological point of view, despite the commerce, culture, and power with which history credits it while Ionian civilization was in the making.  There had been no scientific digging in Lydian soil.  There was no local monument of any importance recognized as Lydian.  No inscriptions, certainly Lydian, had been found in Lydia.  That is enough to say for my present purpose.  To state more fully how Lydia should be related to the Ionian problem, I shall return to it in a subsequent lecture.

And what of the bordering lands on south and north ? The partial excavation of Assarlik had taught us, before 1900, that Aegean influence, or perhaps a few Aegean settlers, had come to Caria towards the close of the Bronze Age and there promoted a derivative culture of an insignificant kind.  More than this, indeed, was to be inferred from Greek tradition ; but there was no archaeological proof.  A little better knowledge had been obtained about the great neighbouring island of Rhodes.  There, too, the earliest local documents, the contents of certain graves at Ialysus, showed participation in the latest development of Aegean civilization ; and the story could be brought down across the dark gap between the Aegean and the Hellenic epochs.  The discoveries made by the brothers Biliotti at Camirus illustrated a productive culture, active in the seventh century B. C. and obviously related to that of the earlier Hellenic period in western Greek lands, including southern Italy, and in Etruria.  But beside this relation, scholars saw another to non-Greek culture, particularly to that of contemporary Egypt.  To account for it they called in Phoenician intermediaries, reminding us how

handily Rhodes lies in relation to the westward sea-ways of
the Semitic folk.  It was the Camirus graves more than
anything else, except perhaps certain discoveries in Cyprus
with which I shall deal later, that led archaeologists to
endorse the common belief in a heavy and various Greek
debt to Phoenicia.

North of the Ionian belt the curious temple-reliefs of
Assos had created the impression that Aeolic Hellenism
had come early into close relation with, and been powerfully
influenced by, non-Hellenic influences; and certain other
discoveries in Mysia, notably the Neandrian volute-capital
and an early Neandrian building, supposed to be a temple,
had strengthened that belief.  The extensive spoil of the
Myrina graves fell almost entirely in an epoch too late to be
instructive as to Ionian origins : but stray objects from
Aeolic coast cemeteries at Cyme, Aegae, and Pitane seemed
to confirm the evidence of Assos.  Whence and how these
Eastern influences, however, came to the Greek settlers,
and how much antecedent culture the latter themselves had
brought over sea, no one pretended to determine.

This last item in the Problem, the cultural equipment
possessed by the early Hellenic colonists at the moment
of their departure from Europe, was the least known of
all the factors.  But before we consider it, let us finish for
the time with Asia by taking summary stock of the knowledge possessed before 1900, concerning the channels through
which influences of Mesopotamia and Egypt must have
passed to Ionia.  It was recognized that, if these influences
came overland, they must have filtered through the area
of a lately rediscovered society of eastern Asia Minor and
northern Syria, which students called the ' Syro-Cappadocian ' or the ' Hittite '.  Links in a possible chain of
westward connexion had been suggested by the observations
of Perrot and Ramsay regarding Syro-Cappadocian features
in the earlier monumental art of Phrygia, and by Sayce's
brilliant inference, based on the rock sculptures of western
Lydia and other monumental and traditional evidence,
that Lydia had once been a ' Hittite satrapy '.  For various

reasons, however, this chain was not regarded as of much importance. Scholars were more inclined to think that Eastern influences reached the coast, if overland at all, through an early north-westward extension of the Phrygian people than through Lydia, which was held to have been comparatively barbarian and insignificant before the establishment of the Mermnad dynasty, early in the seventh century B.C., and to have owed most of its higher culture to reflex influences of Ionia itself. Even Phrygia was regarded as, in her turn, largely indebted to similar reflex influences for the culture which has left us the magnificent rock monuments of the Sangarius basin, and in particular for her alphabetic system of writing ; while a connexion between her early society and the Syro-Cappadocian, though assumed, could not be presented as a certain or momentous factor in the evolution of Western culture, so long as scarce half a dozen widely spaced monuments of Cappadocian character had been detected this side of the Halys and none of Phrygian character on the other side. In fact the whole area of Syro-Cappadocian civilization remained too little known, and its monuments north of the Taurus too few and sporadic, for much weight to be assigned to its influence by those who were speculating on the origin of Western culture. In spite of the repeatedly expressed views of Ramsay, Sayce, Perrot, and others, the ' Hittite ' continued to be envisaged largely as a Syrian civilization which had spread north of Taurus only partially and temporarily, and was more likely to have transmitted its influence by sea through the Phoenicians of Syria than over continental ways of Asia Minor.

To the Phoenicians, indeed, scholars continued to credit the vast bulk of such education as the Greek races were believed to have owed to the East. The advent of their effective influence into the Aegean area was still dated by many far back in the pre-Hellenic period, on the strength of several of the finer objects among Mycenean remains, particularly those which seemed to have reference to cult. Main stations on the westward sea-way of the Semites were

found in Cyprus, Rhodes, and Crete. As for Cyprus, after
the remarkable treasure of Salaminian graves at Enkomi
had come to light, it was seen that the usual assumption of
a Phoenician origin for Cypriote art needed serious revision.
But the continued ascription of many of the finer objects
in that treasure to Eastern sources and a dispute about the
dating of the whole obscured the bearing of its evidence,
although Messrs. Myres and Richter, in their *Catalogue of
the Cyprus Museum* issued in 1899, showed a just apprecia-
tion of the facts. Rhodian archaic civilization was held in
debt to Phoenicia chiefly on the strength of the objects
found at Camirus, which have already been mentioned,
and the Cretan on the strength of the early bronzes extracted
from the Idaean cave. Add to these archaeological observations the strong presumption in favour of Phoenician influence having formed primitive Hellenic art and commerce, which was derived from allusions in Homer, and
statements made by Greek archaeological historians ; from
the early legends of Thebes ; from philological explanations
of the names of those Greek places and divinities which
seemed not to be Indo-European; and last, but not least,
from the yet unquestioned Phoenician origin of the Ionian
alphabet—add all this and it will not appear wonderful that
such protests as were made by M. Salomon Reinach in his
*Mirage Oriental*, and by Mr. Arthur Evans in his first articles
on the Cretan script, did not materially weaken the Semitic
position. Scholars remained content to allow a margin for
Mesopotamian influences transmitted overland through the
Syro-Cappadocian area, and for Egyptian influences exercised
on Greek soldiers and merchants who went from western Asia
Minor to the Nile Valley under the New Empire and thence
returned. But they continued to credit ' the grave Tyrian
trader ' with transmitting at least nine-tenths of the Oriental
stimulus which acted on the nascent culture of archaic
Hellas.

Finally, let us look to the views held about the Ionian
colonists themselves, and the equipment of civilization with
which they were believed to have set sail. There is the less

to say on this head, because there was no very definite view held. Too little, in fact, was known of primitive Greece. There were those, indeed, who argued that the colonization did not all come from Greek ports, but in part from inner Thrace across the straits. Such a possibility, however, threw no light on the precedent culture of the colonists ; for even less was known of primitive Thrace than of primitive Greece. A few archaeologists called attention to the early mid-European culture of the latest Bronze Age and earliest Age of Iron, of which remains had been found in abundance, especially in the upper and middle sections of the Danube basin. Here, they suggested, was evidence that the northern tribes did not descend on Greece from a wholly barbarous area. This fruitful observation however, failed of its full effect, thanks to the rooted pre-judice in favour of deriving the Hellenes directly from an original Asiatic home by way of easternmost Europe, without contamination with mid-European ' barbarians '.

There were others, again, who began to look tentatively to the Mycenean and sub-Mycenean remains of Attica and neighbouring coasts for a solution of this factor in the problem. But even those who held very reasonably that the contents of the early graves at Menidi and Spata, the ' Mycenean ' sherds found in the lowest stratum on the Athenian Acropolis, and the constituent parts of the Aeginetan Treasure, covered the whole period usually assigned to the Ionian colonization, and bore witness to a culture which could not have been without great effect on the colonists ere their departure—even these scholars hesitated to regard Mycenean or sub-Mycenean objects as products of a culture which could have been itself in any part Ionic. To many varieties of creed touching the query, ' Who made the objects called Mycenean ? '—to quote it in Professor Ridgeway's terms—certain articles of belief long remained common, with hardly an exception ; namely, that the makers of those objects and the Ionians were wholly distinct peoples : that the latter came from the north at the end of the Bronze Age ; and that their earliest efforts in art were represented by the geometric 'Dipylon' style which was not in any sense Aegean.

Objections to various articles in this accepted creed concerning the origins of Ionian civilization were obvious and already expressed. The most obvious, perhaps, touched the last article with which I have dealt—the postulate that this civilization owed its inception in large part to colonists of a race which had produced nothing truly artistic in any previous stage of its migrations—nothing, at least, of which actual evidence had been found, despite the fact that in their penultimate stage the colonists had passed across the well-searched soil of Attica. Even if the 'Dipylon' objects could be accepted as witnesses to nascent Ionic art, they seemed to fall in a period subsequent to the colonization. It was generally supposed that the colonists passed on after none but the shortest stay in western Greece and equipped with nothing more than an exceptional 'innate instinct for humanism'. This instinct, encountering on the further shore the fresh and mighty breath of Asia, would be fecundated with a wholly new embryon of civilization.

There is, of course, a measure of truth in this long-accepted theory of the Ionian migration. But a scientific sense trained in the school of evolution cannot but check at the lack of causation and the abruptness of development implied in the explanation as it stood. In particular, one may fairly hesitate to accept 'an innate instinct for humanism' as the sole or even the main asset of a migratory race destined within a very few generations to develop the highest artistic and social culture of the age—a culture, moreover, which was strongly individual. To credit it is, in fact, to be imbued with the spirit of Ottfried Müller and his school of Hellenists—that school which so long denied any alien parentage to Greek culture. Even, nowadays, its prejudice against including the origin of Hellenic civilization among things capable of a scientific evolutionary explanation is not quite extinct. Both in this country and in Germany Hellenism has so far become a cult, that it seems to have votaries still who are slow to admit its obligation to anything but revealed light. The fathering of the Greek on the pre-existing profane cultures has been scouted by perfervid Hellenists in terms which imply that they hold it little else than impiety. Allowing no causation more earthly than vague local influences of air and light, mountain and sea, they would have Hellenism born into the world by a miracle of generation, like its own Athena from the head of Zeus.

Objection was also taken to that article in the accepted creed, which was mainly due to Ernst Curtius, namely, that on the other side of the Aegean the Ionic colonists found a proto-Ionian people, whose near kinship and cultural sympathy went for much in the rapid evolution of the subsequent local civilization. This objection could not, however, be pressed from sheer inability to prove a negative, or even to show much cause in favour of one. To the obvious question, Where were the archaeological remains of these proto-Ionians? was returned the equally obvious and, for the time, sufficient answer that western Asia Minor was most imperfectly surveyed, and its earlier sites had hardly been excavated at all. What material documents of Ionic civilization had we which did not imply a certain degree of adolescence? in particular, for example, what inscriptions which showed forms marking the transition from the parent Phoenician? If documents of infant Ionian culture had not yet been discovered, who doubted that such existed? And if these had yet to be found, so too had the proto-Ionian documents. This answer could not be gainsaid then. It cannot be altogether gainsaid now.

The third main article in the accepted creed, that the Phoenicians acted as the chief transmitters of Oriental influences to Ionia, was the most canvassed of all, because it involved less faith and more knowledge. It was based on the interpretation of a large body of historical data, more or less well ascertained, and was not so much as the other articles dependent on prehistoric probabilities. The Phoenicians, whose credit for influencing Greek civilization had not been great with Ottfried Müller and his followers, came into great vogue with a later school of German historians, of which Büsolt was one of the most able leaders. But in the latter years of the nineteenth century a reaction set in and Semitic claims were often and fiercely challenged. There were felt to be certain potent objections to accepting Phoenician mediation in art at anything like the value set on it by the Büsolt school. Firstly, although the homeland of the Phoenicians itself had long been fairly accessible to students and was rather widely explored in the early sixties, remarkably little evidence of artistic effort had come to light there. If objects of uncertain provenience, which might have been made in other parts of Syria, and early Cypriote antiquities, not found at Kition or at other known Phoenician settlements, were ruled out of court, there was next to nothing left to testify to Phoenician art in the pre-Hellenic age. Secondly, it was objected that so eclectic, so derivative, and so unprogressive an art as was that of Phoenicia, on the showing even of those who claimed for it the widest range of products, was not likely to have exerted much influence on so vigorous and sincere an artistic spirit as was in the early Greeks. Thirdly, many, like Radet when he wrote on Lydia, held justly that possible alternative intermediaries between East and West had not yet been sufficiently considered. The best assured premisses of the pro-Semitic argument did not escape attack. It was counter-argued that the Homeric evidence for the claim had been much overstated, the vast preponderance both of seafaring and of artistic production being ascribed in the Epics, not to Semites, but to Gods or Greeks. Mr. Arthur Evans announced his discovery of an early script in Crete which had nothing to do with the Phoenician system, and more than hinted that he would call in question the supposed debt of Europe to Phoenicia in the matter even of writing. But the Anti-Semites, though fit, were few, and on the whole the Phoenician claim held its own.

What was problematical in 1900 is by no means all well assured in 1908. But in many respects it is better assured. There has been much new light shed, and this I shall try to bring to your notice in the lectures to come. The fresh evidence I propose to deal with in four geographical divisions : (1) Western Hellas ; (2) Hellenic Asia ; (3) Inner Asia Minor ; (4) Syria, with Cyprus and Egypt. It will be, however, neither useful nor, indeed, possible to keep these divisions rigidly separate as so many watertight compartments. The bearing of any particular exploration has often been far from merely local ; and anticipation and recapitulation cannot be altogether avoided.

# LECTURE II

## THE IONIANS BEFORE IONIA

FIRST of all we must arrive, if possible, at some idea of the cultural equipment which the European migrants, credited by unanimous Greek tradition with the main part in the development of Ionian culture, can have taken with them to Asia. We know of two considerable cultures which prevailed before that migration in south-eastern Europe, and seem to have filled all the geographical area out of which it appears the migrants must have come or through which it is certain they ultimately passed. These are the Danubian and the Aegean, to give them convenient geographical names. Both can be followed by their remains from the later Age of Stone, through the Age of Bronze, to at least the opening of the Age of Iron. Is it probable that either or both exercised a formative influence on the Ionians before they left Greece for Asia, and can it be shown that, in fact, they exercised such influence?

To take first the Aegean culture, concerning which by far the most varied and important fresh evidence has come from excavations in Crete. There is neither time nor necessity now to enter upon a detailed description of the discoveries made during these excavations. I must assume your general acquaintance with them, and limit my discourse to an attempt to estimate their bearing on the Ionian problem. Since the Ionian problem is not propounded either by literary tradition or by archaeology before the last part of the second millennium B.C. at the earliest, it will naturally be the latest period of the Aegean Age which will chiefly concern our present inquiry. But there are also certain broad conclusions to be drawn from evidence of earlier Aegean periods, which have important bearing on the matter in hand, and should be stated at the outset, though very briefly.

It need hardly be pointed out that a causative relation between prehistoric Aegean culture and that later historic one, which was developed in the same geographical area, has much greater *a priori* probability, if the former was of great antiquity, of local origin, independent in its development, superior both in aim and ultimate achievement, as ancient cultures go, and in such communication with other high contemporary civilizations as enabled it to share in their progress, than if it had not all or not any of these qualifications.  As a matter of fact, it is proved by its remains to have had them all.

Cretan evidence has established, beyond all possibility of cavil, the aboriginal local character and age-long local development of the Bronze Age culture of the Aegean. There is no longer any question of the latter having been an importation due to alien maritime enterprise and not representative of the aboriginal Aegean society ; nor of its having been so rapidly and sporadically developed as to be without deep social root or more than partial local influence. If there were no other proof, the orderly development of Aegean ceramic art from the most primitive Neolithic ware in unbroken continuity down to the close of the Age of Bronze would alone suffice. Nor is the unbroken series found only in Crete.  At Hissarlik, in the Argolid and in the Cyclades, similar evidence of long-continued ceramic development has come to hand.

Furthermore, we now know that the Aegean civilization has as much right as any, with which it was contemporary, to be regarded as an independent one.  To say this is not, of course, to exclude the effect of foreign influences, about which I mean to speak presently.  A civilization, after reaching a certain height of achievement, never fails to profit by achievements of other contemporary civilizations. As it grows it establishes communications far and wide, and borrows what it wants where it may.  But if at the same time it gives a *quid pro quo* ; if it transforms what it borrows ; if it maintains a distinct individuality in the leading categories of social expression, in its art, for example,

and its system of written communication, then it must be
called independent on any reasonable acceptation of that
epithet.   Such the Aegean civilization remained throughout
its long history.   Its art, whatever alien influence it betrays,
expresses itself from first to last with distinct individuality.
It can always be said of its products, as was said at the
outset by Sir Charles Newton of the so-called ' island stones '
(i. e. certain engraved gems first found in the Cyclades),
that they cannot possibly be mistaken for products of any
other art.   While, as for its system of written communication, no one has ever felt a moment's doubt that it
was of local origin, developed locally out of an independent
pictographic script, and modified during long ages without
reference to any other system.

In the third place, this local and independent civilization
is shown by its monuments to have attained a height of
achievement which entitles it to be set on a par with its
highest contemporaries.   This fact, not made clear before
the Cretan revelations, is of peculiar importance to our
present inquiry, since it must profoundly modify our former
predisposition to look to the Nilotic or Mesopotamian areas
for all the external impulse towards the higher planes of
culture, which classical Mediterranean civilization can have
experienced.   It can hardly be asserted too strongly that
Hellenic civilization, so far from being the first light shed
on barbaric darkness in its own area, was in fact but a re-
illumination, which was long ere it equalled the fullness
of former brightness ;  and that the same soil, in which it
was ultimately to flourish, had already borne a bloom
splendid enough to create cultural influences quite as long-
lasting and stimulating as any of Egypt or Babylon.   Even
if we must suppose this bloom faded or dead before Hellenic
civilization, strictly so called, arose (though how far its
decay had gone and whether equally far in all parts is
still a most open question), the fact of its ever having
reached such excellence introduces a fresh factor into the
Ionian problem.

Finally, we are now in a position to say that intercourse

between civilized continental societies of Africa and Asia on the one hand, and Aegean societies on the other, was far more frequent and close in the prehistoric period than it would be again till comparatively late in the historic age.

On the evidence for relations between the Aegean culture and that of Egypt, from an early period contemporary even with some part of the Old Empire, and culminating under the Eighteenth and Nineteenth Dynasties, I need not dwell. It is well known, and has been set forth lately in sufficient detail in the very accessible work of Professor R. M. Burrows. The cumulative result of that evidence carries conviction to all who have studied the subject. There is a doubt how far back into Egyptian history we may push these relations, and a doubt as to the absolute date of the first epoch at which they appear to have become fully reciprocal, that, namely, of the Twelfth Dynasty. But there is now no doubt whatever of the effective character of those relations henceforward and of their influence on the culture of the middle and later parts of the Bronze Age. Under the first Dynasties of the New Empire, if not earlier, it is clear that the Egyptians and the Kefts of Crete and other Aegean isles and coasts were perfectly well known to each other, maintained direct and constant intercourse, and experienced mutual modification. In a word, the Aegean was open to, and overrun by, Nilotic influences long before the Hellenic period.

Can the same be said of Asiatic influences ? The answer is not so easy and assured. So far, neither have objects undoubtedly Mesopotamian been found on Aegean sites nor objects undoubtedly Aegean in Mesopotamia. But Aegean influence has begun to be suspected in the latter region. Certain ivories found in the early deposit of the Ephesian Artemisium have lately recalled attention to certain others, found forty years ago by Layard in the palace of Senna-cherib at Nimrûd. The latter are in the British Museum, and, always a puzzle to archaeologists, have been labelled Phoenician. They will come up again for consideration later on, and I will only note here that one of the fragments, showing the head of a bull, is as Aegean in style as anything of the Later Minoan art ever found in Crete or the Argolid. Nor is this the only piece which seems clearly to attest some infiltration of Aegean artistic influence into inner Asia. Through what channel that current may have passed I shall suggest in another connexion.

If direct barter of products and influences between the Aegean area and Mesopotamia has left little trace, that is only what is to be expected ; for there were secondary cultures geographically interposed between the two regions. It is more reasonable to look for evidence of communication and intercourse between Aegean society and societies of Syria and Asia Minor. This subject has not yet been worked out ; but already it has been noticed that there are several important features common in a greater or less degree, on the one hand to the Aegean cultural area, and on the other either to the Hittite or to the Syrian Semitic area, or to both. Unfortunately, the west Asiatic societies of the second millennium B.C. are still but very slightly known, and their homelands have not been scientifically searched for those smaller objects of antiquity, which were most generally exchanged, and dropped along trade-routes. The only points, in fact, at which deep excavations have yet been made on sites of the required age lie in Philistia and southern Palestine ; at Sinjerli and Sakjegözu in northern Syria ; and at Boghazkeui in north-western Cappadocia. At Gezer, Tell es-Safi, and other south Syrian sites enough Aegean pottery and weapons and structures of Aegean type have been found to prove that Cretan communication with the south-eastern Levantine shores in the Late Minoan Period was not limited to Egypt—a fact which might, indeed, have been inferred in any case from the tradition which connected the Cretan Minos with Gaza and its cult of Zeus Cretagenes. As for Sinjerli, its pottery and other *Kleinfunde* have not yet been published, although operations ceased on the site not less than fourteen years ago. It is devoutly to be hoped that similar difficulties will not arise to prevent publication of the smaller objects which have been and will be found at Boghazkeui.

Apart, however, from results of Asiatic excavations, there is some very significant evidence that the Aegean and west Asiatic areas exerted influence on each other and were mutually acquainted. Since this evidence bears but on a preliminary point in our present inquiry, I must not do more now than direct your attention to its sources. You will find one source in the early antiquities of Cyprus, as you might expect to do, considering the geographical situation of that island, and particularly in those contents of the Enkomi graves which are now deposited in the British Museum. These objects fall, I believe, very late in the Bronze Age; but they manifestly belong in the main to the Aegean culture, and are local products. Look, for example, at the finest of all the Enkomi objects, the ivory gaming-casket. The hunting-scene carved upon it takes us back without doubt to an Assyrian motive. Not directly, however, but through Syrian imitations, such as the hunting-scene on the Hittite slabs from Sakjegözu, now in Constantinople and Berlin. Yet the motive has been treated as neither a Hittite nor an Assyrian sculptor would have treated it. You will find more evidence in the obvious community of conceptions, held by Aegean religion on the one hand, and by west Asiatic religions on the other; and also in community of symbolism and cult-representation, which is the surer test. If it is much that in both areas the Divine Spirit is made to indwell in sacred trees and pillars, and comes to be personified as a Woman, source and controller of all life, to whom a Son-Consort is given to render intelligible her relation to humanity, it is more that in both areas also the *baetyl* appears in triads and with birds perched atop, that the goddess is attended by lions and set on a hill, that she bears the double-axe, the *bipennis*, as at Cnossus and at Laodicea on the Orontes, and that she stands between animals or birds heraldically opposed, whom she grasps with her hands. You will find yet more evidence in the common use in the Aegean and Asia of singular forms of weapons, such as the shield in the form of a figure of eight ; of singular fashions of dress, such as the flounced skirt ; of architectural plans, such as the Palace disposed round a central court, and of architectural ornaments such as the glazed rosette roundel, with which column bases were veneered in Babylonia and also in Crete ; of artistic conventions such as the representation of a triply-bordered tunic falling in a point between the legs of figures in profile, as at Ivriz and Kara Bel, among Hittite monuments, and on many Aegean gems. You will find, indeed, evidence sufficient by itself to prove close intercourse between Crete and western Asia in objects found by me in 1901 at Zakro—for instance, in those monstrous signet types, made on the spot, which recall the demoniac combinations of Hittite and Mesopotamian cult representation, and in the vases with crescent and disk as relief ornament. Finally, if any doubt remain, consider the evidence set forth by Mr. Evans in the *Numismatic Chronicle* to prove the use of the so-called light Babylonian weight-standard at Cnossus.

We have only to prove intercourse ; and it matters not, for our purpose, in which of the two areas these common features originated. Intercourse is proved by their mere community. But I will remark in passing that the Aegean is as likely to have taught Asia as the reverse. The parallelisms on the Asiatic side are more often to be observed in Assyrian and later Babylonian art than in the earlier Babylonian. Yet it is certain that Aegean art had reached its maturity and begun to decay ere there was any Assyrian art at all, and before there was a Phoenician art which has left us any memorial of itself. If there be any parentage between the Aegean art on the one side and the later west Asian on the other, the Aegean must be accounted the mother art, and responsible for the parallelisms observed in the Nimrûd ivories, and in the earliest pottery and figurines of Phoenicia. These considerations, to my mind, far outweigh that counter-argument, based on the absence of the scarab and the cylinder from Crete, upon which Mr. Evans once insisted. The absence of the scarab would equally disprove intercourse between Crete and Egypt, which is absurd. The absence of the cylinder has little significance, when it is remembered that very few cylindrical seals have actually been found even in Phoenicia—hardly more than, as a matter of fact, have occurred in Cyprus. This very inconvenient form of seal, perpetuated in Mesopotamia owing to lack of stone, was demonstrably supplanted in Syria by conical or gable-shaped forms wherewith the required impress could be made by a single motion of the hand. Yet who would maintain that Syria was not affected by Assyria? I do not say that there was not reciprocity in this matter of influence. It is highly probable there was. Lower Mesopotamia was a seat of considerable culture at least as early as the Aegean; and once communication between the two areas was established through Syrian or Egyptian intermediaries, Babylonian influences would be felt even in Crete. But the balance of influence is in favour of the Aegean. We no longer accept without reservation the old adage, *Ex Oriente lux!*

So much for the earlier evidence tending to show that a native and independent civilization of a very high order, developed in close touch with the Eastern civilizations, had for ages permeated the Aegean area through which the Ionian colonists are supposed to have passed to Asia. Let us look forward and try to discern if traditions or influences of that civilization survived what is usually regarded as the close of the Aegean Age, more particularly in that part of mainland Greece whence was derived the Ionian migration. The evidence for the state of the Aegean area in what has been called the Dark Age is still very scanty and ill-digested. This Age is commonly supposed to have resulted from successive irruptions of comparatively uncivilized northern tribes, strong in the possession of iron weapons, into the area of the old and already decadent Aegean society. The latest and most effective irruption, it is believed, was the Dorian. Certain fresh lights have been cast, albeit somewhat dimly, on this period, partly from Crete, partly from Sparta, which it will be well to consider before we look finally to the Ionic district of Greece.

The upshot of Mr. Evans's examination of the latest remains of the Cnossian Palace, combined with those of a smaller building to the west and the contents of a large cemetery to the north, whose burials were both contemporary with, and subsequent to, the destruction of the Palace, is this.  There was undoubtedly a cataclysmic moment at Cnossus which resulted in wholesale destruction at the end of what is called the Second Later Minoan Period, i. e. about 1400 B.C.  Similar cataclysms, it may be added, seem to have occurred also on all other important Cretan sites yet examined, and at more or less the same moment.  But the Cnossian Palace, and the smaller building to the west of it, were subsequently restored in part and reoccupied by men who continued to use the linear Minoan script as well as domestic and other objects lineally and integrally developed out of the pre-cataclysmic forms.  The Minoan culture, in fact, had so far not been extinguished, nor to any serious extent replaced, or even contaminated, by another in Crete, though reception of Egyptian influence still went on, and a small proportion of northern types of weapons makes its appearance, together with a northern type of house.  It has been shown quite recently in a very able, and on the whole convincing, paper by Dr. Duncan Mackenzie, the learned assistant-excavator of Cnossus, that the explanation of such cultural continuity in Crete, up to the end of the Bronze Age, is to be sought in the probability that the destroyers of the Minoan palaces about 1400 B.C. were not northern 'barbarians', but participants in Aegean civilization pushed out from the mainland by a northern invasion.  Being racially kin to the Cretan Aegeans, these refugees, after overthrowing the Minoan dynasty, settled down without disturbing or modifying the course of Cretan artistic development.  It is on considerably later sites that we first find any evidence of a new cultural element in Crete.  This occurs in certain tombs, belonging apparently to the dawn of the Iron Age.  Here we note that not only iron, but the practice of cremation and the use of the *fibula*, or, rather, of a fashion of dress requiring a brooch for attachment, had come in.   In these tombs, situated towards the east of Crete, there was found in conjunction with weapons not of earlier Cretan forms, but of continental European types, certain pottery already noticed as later than the latest Minoan, by the excavators of Palaikastro.   In this ware a new geometric element of decoration appears alongside earlier Aegean designs and forms.   These tombs and their pottery, Dr. Mackenzie thinks, are to be ascribed to the first ' Hellenic ' immigrants, who came in at the opening of the Iron Age and were probably Achaeans.   The Geometric style becomes rather suddenly thereafter universally prevalent, and the continental types of weapons cease to be exceptional.   This further step must perhaps be ascribed to the subsequent and final wave of immigration, which we call Dorian.   But for my present purpose I wish to insist chiefly on this point. That even in the full ' Dorian ' Geometric ware of Crete Minoan forms and decorative designs play a predominant part.   They have survived, unmistakable, right through the Bronze Age and down into the Iron Age, through the successive invasions of the island by mainland Aegean peoples, by Achaeans, and by Dorians.   In Crete, at any rate, the Hellenic period was cradled among Minoan traditions ; and even if memories of Aegean culture survived nowhere else—an unreasonable supposition— any one discussing hereafter the origins of Hellenism must take account of this fact, that those memories persisted with no inconsiderable vitality in one great Aegean island within sight of the Peloponnese long after the latest date at which the Ionian migrants are supposed to have set sail for Asia.

I turn to Sparta, though with diffidence, since the results of the past season, and indeed many of those of earlier seasons, have been made known as yet only in summary form.   You will be aware that the British Athenian School has been prosecuting researches for the past three years in the precinct of Artemis Orthia, famous as the scene of the experimental flogging of Laconian boys.   Stratum by stratum the diggers have gone downwards, removing in their progress the last vestiges of the reproach so long levelled against Sparta, that she neglected the Fine Arts. These typical Dorians, it now appears, not only had in the sixth century B.C. their local school of rather rigid sculpture, of which a few examples have long been known, but executed, even earlier, as fine carvings in ivory as any of the time, and worked in bronze, clay, and hard stone in a manner equal to the contemporary best. If indeed it be true, as it seems to be from the latest Spartan reports, that the vases, which have long been called 'Cyrenaic', were really of a Spartan fabric developed out of an earlier local ware of 'orientalizing' type, not unlike the early Corinthian, these Dorians were ahead of all Greek potters in the seventh century, and pushed their products even into Egypt.

So much for what the Dorian could achieve, it appears, in the eighth and seventh centuries. But we can now retrace his history farther still. The earliest foundations in the Orthia precinct are remains of a temple in crude brick with wooden framework, whose roof was supported by a single axial colonnade. This structure the discoverers refer to the ninth century B.C. Since a like primitive type has appeared also in Hellenic Asia, at Neandria in the Aeolic Troad, there was thus early some community of tradition between Europe and Asia in the most rigid and conservative of all architectural schemes, that of sacred buildings. To the earliest temple is to be related a great Altar of Sacrifice near by, whose orientation is the same. There were found embedded about its foundations numerous votive objects, the most primitive of which must be referred to an equally remote age; and to these must be added the contents of coeval strata at one or two other neighbouring spots. We have thus, for the first time, a body of documents attesting the art of a mainland branch of the Hellenic race in the ninth century B.C. They consist in chief of painted pottery, ivory or bone fibula-plates, and bronze articles of wear, especially fibulae. Let us see what evidence they offer (so far as their provisional publication can be used) of influences which may have formed Dorian art.

The pottery of earliest Dorian fabric falls into the Geometric class. It is very simple in decoration and finds its closest parallel in certain Geometric ware found on the opposite Adriatic coast, in mid and southern Italy. Geometric ornament of so simple a kind offers no good evidence of derivation, and similar combinations of lines and curves have often, no doubt, originated independently in divers areas. Not having seen the actual sherds in question, I venture to say no more than that the representations already published do not seem to me to preclude such a theory of partial derivation from some late Aegean *Bauernstil*, as certainly holds good in the case of the Cretan Geometric. Late Aegean sherds were found, it appears, on the site of the Amyclaeum, and the Laconian Geometric sherds seem to lie immediately over these. That no Aegean sherds or other things Aegean were found on the Orthia site itself proves no more than that that site was not a sanctuary or an inhabited place in the earlier period of Laconia.

The ivory fibula-plates are more informing. The earliest, which have been published, repeat in more than one case familiar Aegean motives, treated, however, in a manner more Oriental than was used by Aegean artists, and with a new heaviness and grossness of style which is neither Aegean nor Oriental. This style recalls to me very distinctly that of the Bologna *situlae*, the great chased bronze pails of the Villanova period, and also that of some objects among the Idaean bronzes of Crete. The inference that I would draw—though with all apology for rashly drawing any inference at all without having seen the objects in question or possessing more information than is given in provisional reports of the excavation—is this. Two new influences have acted upon a remnant of the Aegean culture, which survived among the subjected Aegean population of Laconia from the period when the Vaphio and Kampos tombs were made. The least important was exercised by Phoenician traders who, as the Homeric poems and Greek tradition recorded,

had been visiting the Peloponnesian coast since the lapse
of the Minoan sea power. This influence drew its inspiration ultimately from Mesopotamian art, but through the
medium of the secondary Hittite culture of northern and
central Syria. The more dynamic influence had come in
with northern iron-using immigrants, who had previously
shared in the important Bronze Age culture of the Danubian
lands. Of this culture more anon. Sufficient to say here
that its remains show it to have been so widely spread over
all the Balkan area and across the broad isthmus between
the Alps and the Black Sea, that it is inconceivable that any
migrants coming from the north at the opening of the Iron
Age could have failed to share it, or at least to have been
influenced by it. It was, beyond question, responsible for
the northern element in the Villanova culture of north Italy,
and equally beyond question it was responsible for the fact
that neither of the two great northern waves, which successively surged over the Peloponnese, consisted of barbarians.
Both the Homeric Achaeans and the historic Dorians of
Sparta must have brought with them both the spirit and the
habit of art. But neither had produced in their northern
homes, so far as we know, anything nearly so fine as these
earliest Spartan ivories. There ensued a surprisingly rapid
advance in their powers so soon as they were settled in
the south, and this we can only ascribe to their education
by the kindred and refined, though decadent, culture of an
older aboriginal population. I must not pursue this fasci-
nating speculation at greater length; but I may just remind
you that Greek tradition always held the Laconian population to be heterogeneous and in great part composed of
subjected elements ; and that, according to the recent
researches of Meister, the true Doric dialect was not spoken
in great part of Laconia.

Finally, the *fibulae* go far to confirm the existence of
a strong northern element in early Spartan society. The
great majority show the double coil or ' spectacles ' form,
which is familiar in Danubian deposits of the Bronze Age,
but not known among purely Aegean remains. Others

replace the bronze coils by plates of bone cut to a similar shape. These occur also on Danubian sites, especially in Bosnia : but they have not been proved to have existed in Aegean lands till the Geometric sub-Aegean period had set in. I found two specimens in the latest stratum of the Dictaean Cave in Crete ; and many occurred in the eighth-century Foundation Deposit of the Ephesian Artemisium.

This, then, is my general conclusion. Dorian art in Laconia was due to the revival of the artistic instincts of an earlier Aegean population by successive bodies of immigrants, drawn from the area of that Danubian Bronze Age culture, which, though kin, had not advanced nearly so far as the Aegean art, nor so seriously exhausted itself. Some further stimulus was imparted rather to the Achaeans perhaps than to the Dorians, by intercourse with Phoenicians, who brought to the coasts imitations of north Syrian art products, or those products themselves. The old Aegean population, however, probably dwindled, and its artistic influence gradually ceased to make itself felt. Hence the remarkable Dorian art of the ninth to the sixth centuries failed in the fifth, and the Spartan, as the recent explorers tell us, became then and thenceforward in reality the artless society which, till lately, we supposed it had been from the beginning.

Now, at last, for the Ionian of Attica. The presumption is strong that his earliest history was, more or less, the same as the Dorian's. Greek tradition derived him from the same ultimate ancestry and the same home ; and Greek tradition of Greek origins, be it noted, has been rather signally vindicated in these latter days. We may trust it so far as to assume that immigrant northerners came down to Attica and neighbouring coasts at the opening of the historic period, and that they were near kin of the Dorians, who had been impelled southwards by more or less the same agencies, whatever those were. We may further assume that, having come under the same cultural influences of central south-eastern Europe, they were by no means barbarians when they eventually descended upon the Hellenic peninsula, but were peculiarly well equipped to understand and assimilate all that remained of the aboriginal high civilization of the Aegean area.

The relations, however, of the two elements which went to make the historic population of Attica seem not to have been the same as in Laconia. We have it on the authority of Thucydides, that the higher class of Athenian society, to which he belonged, held itself to be of aboriginal local stock ; and from the way in which he states this, one would naturally gather that the claim was both one peculiar to the Attic Ionians among Hellenes, and also generally conceded by Hellenic opinion. In Laconia the reverse seems to have been the case. The dominant class was immigrant, but the subjected classes of Perioeci and Helots probably represented older stock. Archaeological evidence goes to indicate that there had survived in the Attic area an unusually late and vigorous bloom of Aegean culture, and one which bears traces of having been affected to an unusual degree by some Eastern influence. I have only to remind those, who have studied 'Mycenaean' remains, of the Spata tombs with their most singular ivories which suggest some art of west Asia, and invite comparison even with Layard's ivories from Nimrûd. The moulded glass and pottery from these tombs seem to date them even later than the so-called ' Re-occupation Period ' of Cnossus, and probably they fall towards the very end of the Bronze Age. At the same time let me recall to you that ' Treasure from One of the Greek islands ' in the British Museum, found as a matter of fact in Aegina. Here again, in the Ionic area, we have very fine work of an even later sub-Aegean style, for which Mr. Evans, when he published this Treasure some years ago, suggested the ninth or eighth century. Like the earlier Late Aegean objects of Attica, these too offer suggestions of Eastern influence, e. g. of Egyptian motives recast, as Mr. Evans said, in a more Oriental mould, and also marked traces of affinity to art of the later Danubian Bronze Age.

In connexion with early Hellenic Attica, however, one must not forget to take into account the evidence of a comparatively rich local Geometric art, following on the decay

of the later Aegean culture. There can be little question
that the so-called 'Dipylon' art was the characteristic
early style of the blended population of this corner of Greece,
and that it owed more to northern influence than to survival
of Aegean artistic tradition, though the latter went for something in its forms and decoration. The natural inference
to be drawn from this fact is, that in Attica the northern
element was even more numerous than in Laconia. But if
due weight be given to the tradition of aristocratic auto-
chthony in Athens, we must suppose that here the older
population was not so much subjected, as in great part
displaced. Perhaps, at first, by far the more numerous, it
tried to subsist on the soil together with the less numerous
but stronger immigrants. But the lean land of Attica
could not long support such increase, and the weaker
elements went presently to the wall, or rather took
to the sea. So we might explain that 'overcrowding of
Athens' which, Greek tradition states, resulted in the
Ionian Migration : and so we should arrive at the logical
inference that the main constituent of the 'Ionian' population, which sailed eastward, was of Aegean race, and
carried Aegean traditions to Asia.

Some element of the northern new-comers, however, there
must have been in that Migration ; or at least, some great
change must have already been worked by them on the elder
population ere it migrated. For without allowing for new
blood, you will account even less satisfactorily for what these
Ionians would achieve in Asia than you will account for
early Dorian art in Laconia if you deny an Aegean sub-
stratum there, and ascribe everything to northern immigrants, who have left no trace in the north of such high
artistic capacity as the earliest Dorian products of Laconia
show. It is doubtless very true that a great deal which was
older, and if you will, 'pre-Hellenic,' coming to the surface
again in Hellas after the tumult of the great Migrations,
eventually determined, in no inconsiderable measure, not
only the development of Hellenic art, but the religious and
political ideas of Hellenic social life. But it must never be

lost sight of that Aegean civilization was demonstrably in
decay when the iron-using races first impinged upon its area ;
and that as a distinct culture, it ran to seed thereafter and
died down.   We know that its growth had covered a very
long time ; but long or short, it was over ; and if the stock
was to sprout anew it could only be after re-fertilization.

In certain cases the renascence of a civilization might
perhaps result from nothing more than fresh external contact
with aliens.   We seem to-day to be watching a case in point
in Japan.   If one were prepared at once to ignore Greek
genealogical tradition, and to credit the Phoenician Semites
with a far more independent, living and dynamic civilization
than there is historic warrant for, one might maintain that
Ionian art was begotten by them on the Aegean culture of
old Attica.   For it is certain that a Semitic expansion did
take place in this Dark Age, thanks to the decline of maritime Aegean power, and that the Phoenician was the one
comparatively fresh influence of the East which we can
follow to the coast of mainland Hellas at this time.   Not
only, however, are the objections to which I have just
alluded, namely, those raised by Greek tradition and the
known character of Phoenician civilization, very strong, but
even Japan does not warrant us in supposing that by mere
contact with alien culture a civilized stock, which had had
so long and so full a growth as the Aegean, could be so re-
fertilized as to produce a new growth of anything like such
freshness and vigour as was the Ionian.   What alone seems
adequate to explain the facts of the case is an infusion of
new blood by a vigorous stock newly come from a more
invigorating clime, but a stock long civilized by a culture
near enough akin to that of the old stock for there to be
ready sympathy between the two.   Otherwise there must
in all likelihood have ensued too long and severe a period
of disintegration for the older and weaker stock to retain
any vigour at all, and for a fresh growth of the higher arts
to have ensued near so rapidly as did the Hellenic bloom
in Ionia.

No sane historian will, I think, now be found to throw

overboard Greek tradition in the matter of the origin of
Ionian civilization. We are bound to believe that the latter
was due in some measure, indeed in great measure, to
colonists from the West, who came over at more or less one
period, not far from the opening of the first millennium
B.C. More than that Greek tradition does not say. If
its statements are carefully compared it will be seen that it
assigns also some share of the credit to peoples previously
settled in Asia and to non-Hellenic civilizations. But more
of this in a later lecture. For my present point it is enough
that some Ionians are to be accepted as having been in
eastern Hellas before there was an Ionia, and that these,
when they passed over to Asia, must have carried a very much
more definite and developed equipment of civilization than a
mere 'innate instinct for humanism'. It seems indeed most
probable that they were themselves a racial blend, whereof
one element, the most vigorous but much the less numerous,
was comparatively freshly derived from south-east central
Europe, where it had participated in a very considerable
Bronze Age culture; while the other, the numerical majority,
was by descent and inheritance representative of one of the
most advanced antecedent societies of the world, one which,
long in close touch with the ' living East ', had assimilated
into its own system no small part of the East's social progress.
What the Ionian took to Ionia was a fusion of the Danubian
with the Aegean culture. This would develop a fresh growth
on a new soil, which lay more open to vital influences of the
East than any on which either culture had flourished theretofore. There is no ' miracle ' about Ionian civilization;
but there is a good deal yet to explain.

# LECTURE III

## IONIA

WHEN summarizing knowledge about the origins of Ionian civilization up to 1900 in my Introduction, I said that the most serious difficulty in determining its component elements arose from lack of archaeological evidence about Ionia before the Ionians. That difficulty, unfortunately, remains to this day little lessened. If the ruined tumulus near old Aeolic Smyrna, known as the Grave of Tantalus, and certain rude and half-buried traces of primitive inhabitation and human handiwork near it and on the mountain behind, had then to bear obscure and solitary witness to the pre- or proto-Ionians in Ionia itself, their witness is not more illuminating now. For neither have they been re-examined, nor has anything bearing on them come to light elsewhere. Until scientific excavation is made and potsherds and other small objects are found, either in that tumulus itself or in the settlement near it, it must remain quite doubtful to what people or date it is to be assigned. It may have been made by such a proto-Ionian race as the Thraco-Phrygians or the Leleges, or by the hands, whether Cappadocian or Lydian or what not, which carved the sculptures on the neighbouring rocks of the Kara Bel by Nymphi; or it may not be pre-Ionian at all. In any case the rock sculptures of Nymphi and Sipylus remain our most significant material witnesses to a pre-Ionian civilization, whether of native or foreign origin, in the central coast-land of western Asia Minor. I shall speak again of them presently.

The literary testimony of Greek tradition and belief on this matter is more suggestive than explicit. In Homer no cities on the west mainland coast are mentioned as Greek, but Miletus is alluded to as a town of the ' barbarous-speaking Carians ' Several of the southern islands, however, join the Achaean forces ; and in Rhodes in particular, Lindus, Ialysus, and Camirus appear as presumably Greek cities. One never likes to rely on Homeric silence. There is a good deal of reason to doubt whether the authors of the Homeric lays knew much about any part of Asia Minor except the extreme north-west corner. I say this with full consciousness that those lays have often been held of Ionian origin. But this theory runs contrary to the mass of the internal evidence. The diction of the lays, the geographical equipment of their authors, the social setting and the traditional relations of the leading characters, all point to a Western origin. What the epic authors knew of Asia they learned in all probability, at second-hand, from those who made such raids on its coast as that with which the *Iliad* itself is concerned. Something more may have been derived from errant bodies of Achaeans like those Aquaywâsa, who joined other ' Peoples of the Sea ' in attacking Egypt, about 1180 B.C. But it did not amount to much. The epic authors had, however, heard positively of Miletus at any rate as an existent city, a city of the Carians, who spoke a tongue unknown to the Achaeans, and were expert in such a delicate art as the tinting of ivory.

This being so, it is interesting to turn to the site of Miletus itself, and ask how far the excavations, prosecuted there since 1900 by Dr. Theodor Wiegand, for the Berlin Academy of Sciences, have cast any light on a Carian origin of the city. This exploration has been directed chiefly, like so many other German excavations in Asia Minor, to architectural ends and, therefore, on a great part of the site has been limited to the clearing of ruins of the more important public buildings of the Imperial Age. But at a few points the explorer has been able to penetrate lower and to open out remains of earlier times, notably in and about a small shrine of Athena whose foundation goes back to the seventh century B.C. at least, and probably earlier. Hereabout, as I understand (for there has been as yet no full publication of the early remains), he unearthed certain traces of prehistoric structures and a small number of fragments of Aegean vases lying on the virgin soil. I have never seen them, but Mr. Cecil Smith, who has done so, confirms their Aegean character. I gather that they belong to a very late epoch—*spätmykenisch*, Dr. Wiegand calls them. Probably they are not earlier than the Ialysus vases from Rhodes, or those from Assarlik in Caria, which, being associated with iron weapons, represent the very end of the Aegean period. So far as they go, however, these sherds attest the existence of a settlement on the site of Miletus prior to the accepted date of Ionian colonization.

This is very slight material evidence, and one had hoped for much more. But so far as it goes, it distinctly supports the inference drawn from Homer that there was a civilized Miletus before the Ionians appeared—an inference which is in accord, moreover, with the indication given by a story of Herodotus concerning the Carian wives of the first Greek settlers. There are also other allusions to pre-Ionian Carians in what was to become Ionian territory—for example, those who, according to Pausanias, were found by Androclus and his band of colonists, living in sanctuary with Leleges and Lydians about the Ephesian *hieron*. We need not attempt here to answer the question, who were these Carians ? Ramsay and others have shown that the historic people of that name was compounded of at least two elements, one of which was Indo-European ; and there was a persistent Greek tradition which connected Carians with early Crete and the pre-Hellenic period in the Cyclades. Sufficient for our present purpose that they were present as, apparently, a civilized people on the west-central Anatolian coast ere the first Ionian migrants arrived. If the evidence of excavation at Miletus, Assarlik and Ialysus is to go for anything, they had been reached by, or had perhaps imported, the Aegean culture of the very latest Bronze Age.

If we could be more sure of the high antiquity of Biblical references to *Javan*, we should have to suppose that the Ionian name was in Asia before the Ionian Migration. If so, earlier migrants must have brought it across the Straits.

But there is no necessity so to antedate it. The first Biblical reference which we can use with any confidence is that in Ezekiel concerning the supplying of iron to Syria by Javan ; and this applies to as late a period as the seventh century. The supposed Egyptian reference to Ionians in the Hittite Confederacy of the fourteenth century B.C., based on Champollion's reading of the poem of Pentaur, has long been discredited.

On the whole, then, scanty Greek tradition and scantier monumental evidence from Ionia itself, taken together, tend to indicate pre-Ionian inhabitation of the west-central Anatolian coast by heterogeneous, weak and scattered, but not uncivilized populations. These seem to have been loosely dominated at the earliest epoch, of which we have any knowledge, by the inland Syro-Cappa-docian power, and subsequently perhaps, in some measure, by another inland power, which rose out of the decay of the first, namely, the Phrygian. To the latter the Tantalid legends of Aeolic Smyrna seem to attach : to the former, the rock monuments of Sipylus and Nymphi.

One or both of these inland powers, however, there is some reason to think, was strong enough on the west coast, to keep it from having any political connexion with the Aegean centres of civilization, and perhaps from being affected by Aegean culture till almost the end of the Aegean Age. When, on behalf of the British Museum, I re-explored, in 1904–5, the site of the great shrine of Artemis at Ephesus, I ascertained an important negative fact. In the large area occupied by the platforms of the successive temples, not less than five in number, which were raised on this site, I penetrated to the virgin sand over almost all the central space upon which the three earliest (and smallest) of those temples stood, and I found a very rich deposit of votive objects and various fragments, including a good deal of pottery, in the lowest stratum of all. But I got not one sherd of Aegean ware, nor any article of true Aegean fabric, nor indeed anything of the subsequent so-called Geometric style, except two minute fragments of a vase. Yet there is no possible doubt that I reached the bottom of human remains on the site. My lowest stratum was bedded evenly upon clean saturated sand, evidently the surface of a fluvial marsh, whose upper level lay not two metres above that of the distant sea, and considerably below the present bed of the Cayster river at its nearest point. Into this sand, which lay more than a metre below the level of saturation in early summer, and could only be examined by continually exhausting the infiltration with a steam-pump, five-foot probes could be driven up to their heads at all points without encountering the least resistance. Beyond question this is the original marshy ground on which, as Pliny tells us, the earliest Artemisium was founded in the hope that it would enjoy comparative immunity from the effects of earthquake.

It is always difficult to prove, and dangerous to press, negative evidence in archaeology. An earlier settlement than the earliest which I found, may very well have existed on another part of the large space afterwards regarded as the *hieron* of Artemis. For nothing but the rectangle, some one hundred metres by sixty, occupied by the great temple itself, has been examined to the bottom or anywhere near it. Or the earlier *hieron*, around which the first Ionian colonists found a mixed native population living ἱκεσίας ἕνεκα, may not have lain anywhere near the later Artemisium, but have been that Ortygian shrine of Leto in the hills to the south, which later tradition seems to have regarded as the mother church. If Pliny's story of the earliest Ionian foundation and the reasons of its location is true, it implies that a fresh site was selected, not likely to have been chosen by earlier builders.

Nevertheless this negative result of my deep excavation of the Artemisium is not without significance. It tallies with the almost equally negative result, as regards earlier Aegean things, which has thus far followed on all exploration whatever in Hellenic Asia, both mainland and isles, except only at Hissarlik. For all the rest of the coast, as has been already said, we have nothing at all that is Aegean to

record, except vases or sherds of the very latest Age of
Bronze or earliest of Iron, found at three points only on
the mainland, viz. Pergamum, Miletus, and Assarlik, and at
one point in Rhodes.  The last named island has been
scoured of late by successive exploring parties, British and
Danish, in search of things Aegean, but nothing earlier than,
or even as early as, the Ialysus vases can be discovered
on its surface.  True, there has been no further Rhodian
excavation, except one in historic strata at Lindus.  But
nowhere else, where Aegean things have eventually been
unearthed in any abundance, as e. g. in Cyprus, Crete, or
the Argolid, have explorers, consciously searching for
Aegean remains, drawn the surface so blank.  It certainly
!ooks as if Rhodes had not received its western settlers
long before the date of the *Iliad*.  The other great islands
near the Ionian coast, Samos, Chios, and Mitylene, have
yet to produce a single well-attested Aegean object.

There is, therefore, perhaps, just enough reason to hold
as a working hypothesis that, except for their north-western
corner, the Asiatic coasts of the Aegean lay, until very late,
outside the culture-area associated with the name of that
sea.  But if 'tis true, 'tis strange !  Why did the Cretan
and other Aegean sea-rovers, whether pirates or merchants
or both, fail to settle on these particular coasts and isles ?
They had pushed their wares into Hissarlik, and had filled
all the opposite shores of Europe with a culture much higher
and more vigorous than any which has left a contemporary
trace in Anatolia.  I can conceive but one reason which will
explain such a fact, if fact it be ; and that is this.  There
must have been some strong continental Power dominating
all the west-central coast of Asia Minor from an inland capital.
It must have been a non-maritime Power, careless about
developing its coast lands, but careful to keep others away
from them.  In fact some Asiatic race was playing thus
early the same part, and was producing the same result in
Anatolia that, in the historic age, first the Mermnad kings
of Lydia, and later, during two epochs, the Achaemenid kings
of Persia, played and produced.  But with this difference.

These historic Powers came to the front after a period of disintegration, during which numerous alien cities had come into being on the western coast. They had thus to occupy and dominate an existent coastal civilization already in full growth. But that prehistoric dominant Power came before this period, and found at most but a few weak cities on the coasts to take or leave. It was not studious to create more. Remember that, throughout history, the rich littoral districts of Asia Minor have always fallen to continental Powers of Asia, unless there were a very strong maritime Power of Europe which desired them. They have never stood long independent in their own strength, or been able to withstand Asia, while the maritime peoples of south-eastern Europe were weak. Geographical situation and climatic conditions are constantly detrimental to their Europeanism. Their territories lie, rich and enervated, at the foot of easy roads, leading down from another and a more virile world.

It need not, however, be supposed that, if such an inland power existed and cried hands off to would-be settlers and raiders, it had no relations at all with the sea-rovers of the Aegean. Some measure of commercial intercourse there may well, and indeed there must, have been, quite sufficient to account for the passing of mutual influence from the sea to the continent, and the continent to the sea. What this Power may have been and where centred, I will inquire in another discourse, when I come to consider what lay to the east of Ionia. I pause here only to say that my supposition involves, of course, a corollary. The inland Power in question must have grown weaker late in the Aegean period, and have so far been broken up before 1000 B. C., that the western coasts, formerly closed, became open to hardy adventurers. If later on I can show that there was actually a strong inland Power in Asia Minor which did suffer conspicuous decline or disintegration at about that epoch, I shall have established a fair prima facie case.

If our present documents for Ionia before the Ionians

are but little better than those available ten years ago,
are we better off for documents illustrating the beginnings
of the subsequent period, traditionally associated with
a migration from the west ?   The earliest remains on
the Artemisium site at Ephesus comprise, as I have just
said, nothing that can be referred to local pre-Ionian
civilization.   But they do offer a good deal of inferential
evidence upon the course of the subsequent archaic Ionian
development.   Indeed it is in considering them, that
archaeology has obtained the first clear view of the historic
Ionian civilization in the making.   Some archaic Ionian
evidence has been obtained also at Miletus.   But, so far
as I have been able to learn, the Milesian documents for
this period are much less numerous and significant than the
Ephesian.   In any case, they cannot safely be used till they
are finally published by their discoverer.   I shall devote
myself, therefore, to the Ephesian, on which I can speak
at first hand.   I have stated the circumstances under which
I found these documents, and have given a detailed catalogue
in a volume lately issued by the Trustees of the British
Museum.   I need recapitulate the main facts but very
briefly.   When I went to Ephesus in 1904, I was com-
missioned, among other things, to probe beneath the temple
platform constructed in the sixth century B. C., and exposed
in 1870 by J. T. Wood, who regarded it to the end of his
life as the earliest structure on the site.   It seemed, however,
unlikely that a sanctuary so greatly honoured by all the
Asiatic Hellenes had its origin thus late in their history.
After clearing that platform once again and more thoroughly,
and piercing it in vain at several points of its outer periphery,
I began to examine a rectangular marble foundation in its
axial centre, the top of whose highest course, lying a little
lower than the *cella* pavement, had been revealed by Wood.
The latter believed it to be the sub-structure of an internal
Great Altar, but did not explore it farther.   On beginning,
however, deeper clearance around and inside it, I found
not only that there was but one course of marble and that
below this began faced masonry of other stone, unlike that

used in the sixth-century temple, but also that a part of the rectangle was filled in solid with evenly-laid slabs of limestone compacted with mud mortar.   On lifting the upper slabs I came upon numerous pieces of jewellery in gold and electrum, and other personal ornaments and articles of wear in ivory and other materials.   These were for the most part so perfect in every detail, that it is incredible that they could have been puddled up unseen in mud mortar and dumped as rubbish where they were ultimately found.   The only possible alternative is to suppose that they were carefully laid between the slabs for some hieratic purpose, for example, as a foundation deposit, intended, according to the original motive of all such deposits, for the fruition of the deity of the shrine.   In all likelihood the structure containing this deposit was not an altar at all, but the Basis of the central cult-statue of the Ephesian Goddess.   If the foundations at central points of other Greek temples were laid open now (e. g. in the Parthenon, and the Delphic and Olympian shrines), I believe it would be found that it was the Hellenic practice to hide foundation deposits under the central statue.

To make what might be a long story short, I will only add that the progress of the clearance, carried on with great difficulty in water and slime with the aid of pumps, ultimately showed that this central Basis had been twice enlarged by additions on all sides except the western.   The original and smallest rectangle, based on a slab foundation, bedded about two metres below the sixth-century pavement in clean marsh-sand, was built in fine early masonry of green schist, faced on the outer sides only.   On the inner faces the blocks were left rough and bonded into the slab-filling. This filling, without which the structure was not compact or stable, continued, as it was removed layer by layer, to produce jewellery and other small objects, identical in style throughout.   But it was productive only within the area of the smallest and earliest rectangle.   The filling of the later enlargements on three sides contained practically nothing except a possibly sacrificial deposit of bones and charcoal

in one angle.  The total number of objects in precious
metals, ivory, bone, paste, crystal and other materials,
found in the smaller rectangle, was a little above one thousand ; and, with the exception of twenty-eight electrum
coins, these objects were trinkets or other articles of personal
wear or cult use.  In the latter category must be reckoned
a number of artificial *astragali*, made in ivory and variously
decorated.  These were probably used for divination or
dedicated as tokens after successful appeal had been made
to the oracle with natural knucklebones, of which some also
were found in the same deposit.

The inevitable inferences from these facts, as they present
themselves to me, are these.  The smallest rectangle is the
earliest, and as early as any structure on the site.  Its
slab-filling was coeval with it, and the objects in that filling
were placed there carefully as the structure was being built.
They too, therefore, are as early as anything on the site.
Subsequent to this foundation, but before the middle of the
sixth century, two successive restorations of the Basis have
to be allowed for.  The smallest rectangle must, therefore,
antedate the epoch of Croesus by a considerable space of time.

Continuing my exploration of the lowest strata round
about this Basis, I found, corresponding to its three periods,
structural remains of three primitive temples.  All were
small and contained within the space occupied later by no
more than the *cella* of the sixth century ; and all had the
Basis for their central point.  The pavement level of each
successive temple was raised above the last ; but the third
and highest primitive pavement lay rather less than one
metre below that of the great temple of the sixth century.
The third primitive structure was the largest and the only
one whose ground plan was sufficiently preserved for its
form to be conjectured.  It seems to have been a temple
*in antis* of the usual Hellenic proportions, facing west, without
peristyle, and built of fine limestone, not marble.  Whether
it had a single axial row of columns, like the early Ionic
shrine at Neandria, or the first temple of Artemis Orthia at
Sparta, no traces remained to show ; but probably it had.

In the area occupied by these three primitive temples, but in the bottom stratum of deposit, which alone had escaped disturbance at the hands of those who laid the foundations of the great sixth-century platform, I found some two thousand more small votive objects and fragments. The great majority of these can be referred certainly to the same period as the Basis Treasure, in virtue either of intrinsic similarities, or of the relation in which they lay to primitive foundations. They included some sixty more electrum coins and several pseudo-Egyptian scarabs, besides a number of fine ivories, and a good deal of bronze, a metal almost completely absent from the Basis Treasure. As a whole, however, the articles found outside the Basis were in much smaller proportion personal trinkets, and were less well preserved.

This collection of about three thousand objects and the earliest Artemisium, to which they seem almost without exception to have belonged, form the body of evidence on which I propose to draw. I date the objects about the end of the eighth century B. C., partly in consideration of the interval reasonably to be allowed for the succession of three temples, one over another, before the middle of the sixth century; but more by comparison of other finds made elsewhere, which offer analogies of fabric and style. Especially to be compared are those gold objects from Camirus in Rhodes and the Polledrara tomb at Vulci in Tuscany, which are dated, by their association with scarabs of Psammetichus I, with probability to the latter half of the seventh century, but seem products of a slightly more advanced art. The Treasure in the Ephesian Basis I hold to have been put there intentionally at the moment of the original foundation, not much later or earlier than 700 B. C. The objects found outside are probably remains of votive and other possessions of the earliest temple, dedicated during its apparently short life, and, for the most part, broken and trampled at some cataclysmic moment into the slime of what has evidently been always a very wet site. This moment occurred very possibly during that Cimmerian raid on Ephesus which

Herodotus and others record as having happened in the reign of Ardys II of Lydia.

Here, then, is a body of documents speaking to Ionian civilization, as it was some two centuries after the traditional landing of the western colonists. Of course, all the documents need not speak to that moment only. Some may well be of an earlier date, heirlooms from previous generations, given up at last to the goddess when the site in the plain, to be peculiarly associated with her thenceforward, was first chosen for her shrine. Trinkets of all kinds, especially those in metal, are apt to be long preserved in use. Some of those found in the Artemisium—the bronze *fibulae* for example—show various stages of development, from simple bows on which beads of amber or composition were strung, to heavy bows on which solid mouldings imitate those adventitious embellishments. Among objects of another class, also, erect female statuettes, of which probably several represented the goddess (but perhaps, as Mr. Cecil Smith prefers, her votaries), there is evidence of development. One can trace progress from very rudely modelled figures, terminating below in columnar form without indication of feet or indeed of any human shapeliness, to the exquisitely carved but still archaic and faulty form, represented on the cover of the British Museum book. The possibility of the variations being due to difference of contemporaneous fashion or difference of individual craftsmen's skill should not, of course, be excluded. But these explanations of variation are the less probable in a matter of early handiwork.

In any case the elaborate design and execution of most of the Ephesian documents, notably the trinkets and jewels in electrum, imply a long previous evolution of skilled craft. How long had it been proceeding in Ionia itself ? Can it, in any case, be supposed to have begun there, or are the ancestors of the Ephesian objects to be looked for elsewhere ? These questions cannot, perhaps, be satisfactorily answered yet. But there are certain considerations which may help towards an ultimate answer.

When I came to catalogue and compare the Ephesian documents, I found myself recurring again and again to the Enkomi Treasure, which was discovered in graves near Salamis in Cyprus, and is now almost all lodged in the British Museum. I had, thus far, followed certain very competent critics of Dr. A. S. Murray's publication of that Treasure, in holding it to be some eight centuries earlier than the earliest date to which the Ephesian objects could possibly be assigned. Those critics had referred it to the period of the Mycenae shaft-graves. On re-examining it, however, in the light of evidence which was not available when those criticisms were written, since it has been collected largely by the subsequent labours of the chief critic himself, Mr. A. J. Evans, I found myself dating it a good deal later. There may be some confusion of earlier and later burials, or certain of the trinkets may have survived, as trinkets will, from an earlier Aegean period, the second Late Minoan. But most of the objects which are not likely to have been heir-looms, such as the pottery and some bronzes, seem clearly to be as late as, or later than, the Reoccupation Period at Cnossus. Indeed, they are fully as late as the Ialysus objects from Rhodes. I am now prepared to subscribe to the epithet ' sub-Aegean ', which more than one authority has applied to the Enkomi Treasure. If the mass of it is to be referred, then, to the very end of the Bronze Age, the interval of time which divides it from the Ephesian Treasure is not so very great.

The analogies between the two Treasures are many and striking. One notes them in fabric, as in the fashioning of hollow figurines in two plates, front and back ; in form, as in the spiral shape of ear-drops, the high arch of ear-rings, and in the types of certain *fibulae*, pendants and beads ; in design, as in the bead-clusters and the use of almost identical tiny animals, human heads, and insects as pendent attachments to necklaces and ear-rings ; in pattern, as in the use of the bow-coil in various combinations, and in the frequent dog-tooth disposition of soldered granular decora-tion. A significant parallel in artistic convention is seen in sphinxes which have a spiral frontal lock of hair.  This latter feature, like the bow-coil, may be of Mesopotamian origin. But, since it appears also on sphinxes found both among the Spata ivories, and in a tomb at Cnossus, which is apparently of the third Late Minoan period, it had evidently been domiciled so long in the Aegean area, that one cannot reasonably suppose that the Ephesian goldsmiths derived it independently from the East.  In fact, a good many of the Oriental traits, which we shall notice presently in the Ephesian work, are anticipated by the Enkomi Treasure. I shall return to the latter hereafter when discussing so-called Cypro-Phoenician art.  Enough to say now that the bulk of the Enkomi objects are Cypriote and not Phoenician, and that their inspiration is due obviously to Aegean art.  The Ephesian objects, on the other hand, are certainly not Cypriote.  There is ample presumption from the presence of goldsmiths' refuse in the temple itself, and from the frequent occurrence of certain peculiar forms and decorative motives, for example, the bee, that this Primitive Treasure was, in the main, made at Ephesus itself.  But equally certainly its constituents, with few exceptions, seem to me to be related essentially to the same system as the Cypriote, i. e. to the sub-Aegean culture, even if their relation be more remote.

Naturally, however, if that be the case, it is not among the Cypriote Aegean things only that one ought to note Ephesian analogies.  How about Hissarlik, the one important Aegean site yet explored in Asia Minor?  Any one who takes the trouble to read through my catalogue of the Ephesian Treasure will find almost as many comparisons noted with Hissarlik as with Enkomi.  I do not press them, however, to the same extent, because the Hissarlik documents in question were almost wholly found by Schliemann's workmen in those strata above the ' Burnt City ', which were notoriously ill-observed and often confused by the observers, before Dörpfeld came to the rescue of the site.  The many forms and designs, parallel to, and sometimes identical with, the Ephesian, are to be ascribed in some cases possibly to the sixth city, and in more to the seventh and eighth. In many cases they may be evidence of a culture rather contemporaneous with, than prior to, the Ionic Ephesian. But at Hissarlik Aegean traditions are more than likely to have inspired every stage of archaic culture.

With the products of the western Aegean societies such close parallelism is not to be looked for. These are in very great proportion of much earlier date, or, if of anything like the same period, represent an art which was developed (according to my hypothesis of Ionian origins) without so much exposure to alien influences as the Ionian and the Cypriote. But, nevertheless, the Ephesian objects present many points of analogy with the later mainland Aegean remains at Mycenae, Spata and other sites. One notes at Ephesus the continued vogue of several ' Mycenean ' fashions, e.g. of circular plaques of precious metal with engraved or stamped patterns, often of distinctly sub-Aegean character, which were sewn on to textiles to form the enrichment of diadems or robes ; of clear white rock-crystal, esteemed apparently one of the most precious substances in the Aegean period ; of the *labrys* or double war-axe as a decorative motive ; of the heraldic opposition of animals in decorative cult-schemes ; of the use of insects in precious metal for pendants ; of clusters of soldered beads ; and finally of polychromy in ceramic decoration. This Middle Minoan fashion emerged again conspicuously in later Ionian pottery, as discoveries at Eleusis, Rhodes, and especially Naukratis, sufficiently prove.

If we look, on the other hand, for traces of the other original ingredient in the equipment of the Ionian colonists, the culture of mid-Europe, we find them indeed clear and distinct, but much less frequent. We find them, for example, in the *fibulae*, as indeed we should expect to do if the ' safety-pin ' *fibula* had come to Greece from the north. It is not by their form so much that the Ephesian *fibulae* remind us of the mid-European area. The majority of the Ionian specimens are of that simplified type, called by Furtwängler *kleinasiatisch*, which appears, from its comparative rarity in deposits on the west of the Aegean, to have been developed on the eastern shore, and to have made its way into inland fashion. But it is by their adventitious ornament, which consisted mainly of beads threaded on the bow. These beads (sometimes very shapeless) were generally of amber, and apparently of Baltic amber. Like the *fibula* itself, I take this fashion of bead ornamentation to be of mid-European origin. It has left traces of itself on most archaic Greek and Graeco-Etruscan sites. A peculiar parti-coloured and three-cornered bead in compost, with boil-like protuberances, which has been found in quantities both at Ephesus and in archaic Greek strata elsewhere, often took the place of amber on the *fibula* bow. Beads of similar character and colouring were found in early Bronze Age tombs at Jezerine in Bosnia. Let me call attention also to another *fibula* ornament, found at Ephesus many times over, the double ivory plate of ' spectacles ' form. These are a very common Bosnian addition to the *fibula*, but have been but rarely found elsewhere, although double coils of metal, making similar ' spectacles ', have occurred often enough in archaic Greek strata. A curious metal bead, cylindrical, swelling in the centre, variously ornamented with moulded rings, and pierced longitudinally, which appeared in both precious metal and bronze at Ephesus, takes us back to the Hallstatt graves.

It is remarkable, however, and I think very significant, that, from a large class of common toilet articles found at Ephesus, one mid-European form, preponderant on archaic Greek sites of the west, is wholly absent, namely, the pin with flat disk or spool for its head and spool-like enlargements and mouldings on the upper part of the shaft. This adds one to the many pieces of evidence which tend to show that in Ionian civilization the mid-European element was less strong, and the Aegean element more strong, than in either the Dorian or the Ionian culture of the west. But that these two are the elements out of which, in whatever proportion, Ionian art was originally compounded, the whole mass of the Ephesian evidence, in my opinion, goes strongly to prove.

I will leave to my final lecture the attempt to suggest at what period or periods, and in what manner, these two main elements came to Asia Minor in the Ionian Migration. But a *caveat* may be entered here against any assumption that either or both elements were entirely absent from Asia before that Migration. There is reason to believe both that some population, racially kin to that which developed the Aegean culture, was present on the Anatolian coasts from early times, and also that there had been very early passage of influences and perhaps of peoples, from Balkanic Europe to Asia Minor. Not only has the earliest sub-neolithic stratum at Hissarlik produced pottery and weapons closely resembling those of neolithic Danubian graves, but at two other places, where sub-neolithic settlements have been explored in north-west Asia Minor, Danubian analogies are even more certainly to be remarked. These places are Boz Eyuk in central Phrygia, and Yortan in Mysia. The vases of the latter site, where is a cemetery of the earliest Bronze Age, show close analogies with Cypriote forms and suggest that the earliest migrants from Europe spread sporadically far down through the peninsula to the Levant. That their intermediate stations between north Phrygia and Cyprus are not known, does not prove that such did not exist ; for no attempt has been made to explore sub-neolithic sites in any other part of the peninsula.

There remains, however, a new element to be considered in the evolution of Ionian civilization. In the stage at least at which the Ephesian documents reveal it, it had experienced also divers influences neither mid-European nor Aegean. It is comparatively easy to point out the effect of these. The difficulties thicken, when we try to determine whence and by what road they came, and especially whether any of them represent a culture which was in Ionia before the Ionians.

A most important class of Ephesian documents betrays

especial influence of the East, namely, the ivory statuettes of human and animal forms. Ivory, as a material, always suggests the East, but in this connexion it must be remembered that during a long previous period it had been known and used in the Aegean area. Witness the statuettes and plaques of Cnossus, the plaques and figurines of Spata, and the gaming-casket and other objects of Enkomi. Although, in the Homeric poems, the tinting of ivory is not alluded to as a Greek art, the Ephesian ivory statuettes are without doubt Ionian work. As Mr. Cecil Smith pointed out, in publishing the finest of them, the finely engraved patterns on certain of the dresses correspond closely with the decoration of painted pottery found on the site and indubitably Ionian. It may be added that they correspond also with textile patterns painted on fragments of large archaic marble sculpture from the Temple. Furthermore, several of the female figures wear distinctively Greek dress, and one carries in her hands distinctively Greek vessels. These considerations are enough to prove the point without calling in an argument from style which must ultimately be based on the somewhat later Ionian art-remains hitherto known to us. Since these themselves were possibly derived from the school which produced these very ivory statuettes, any inference from them might be held to involve us in a vicious circle. Ionian though they are, the Ephesian ivories recall, in both general and particular characteristics, artistic work of inner Asia. They show the same general tendency to conceal poverty of modelling under formless drapery, elaborate surface-ornament and meticulous treatment of external details : they show similar particular conventions in the treatment of animal muscles and animal hair. The general style of the lion-statuettes is that of Babylonia or early Assyria : an individual winged sphinx has panel-work in relief on the forelegs, a peculiarly Assyrian feature. Several of the smaller ivories, too, show fashions of the East rather than of the Aegean. The goddess, in an exquisite little ivory relief, holding two lions in heraldic pose, is winged : a miniature chariot-wheel has the eight spokes of Mesopotamia : a stud, with human face in relief, is of a peculiar form found before only in Babylonia; the lotus-leaf and bud pattern, used on an inlay strip and on a roundel, is the derived and improved Mesopotamian variety of an originally Egyptian motive ; a double comb reproduces exactly a peculiar Mesopotamian form, while the simplicity of its ornament is in Greek taste. I need not weary you by accumulating proof of a fact which is not disputed. But I must call your attention to one point more. It was first noticed by Professor Sayce, I believe, that as a whole these Ionian statuettes present the closest and most various points of stylistic similitude to those ivories found by Layard at Nimrûd, whose Aegean affinities I have already mentioned. Their points of resemblance to the Ephesian ivories enumerated by Mr. Cecil Smith (to whom belongs the credit of following up Professor Sayce's suggestion) are even more remarkable. He noted identity in the general treatment of the draped human form, with its elaborately minute surface detail and very summary modelling, and in the particular treatment of the eye, which is shown always at Nimrûd and often at Ephesus with hollow drilled iris and harsh deep grooves for eyebrows. Two human figurines, one bearing distaff, the other a supposed eunuch priest with official chain, and both wearing high cylindrical headgear, stand in very close relation, in both style and attributes, to Nimrûd objects : while the dress of several of Layard's figurines, including a πότνια θηρῶν who is wingless as in Aegean art, is hardly distinguishable from the early Greek.

Mr. Cecil Smith was so greatly impressed by this parallelism that he has proposed an actual Ionian origin for the Nimrûd ivories. This suggestion, if accepted, would modify seriously the problem of the origin of Ionian art. Two facts are incontrovertible about the Nimrûd ivories. First, both the circumstances of their discovery and their style demand their ascription to at least a century earlier than the Ephesian ivories. Second, with all their Aegean and

Ionian affinities, they are very distinctly more Oriental in subject, style, and treatment than anything Aegean or Ionian yet found.    On Mr. Smith's supposition we stand, as we look at the Nimrûd ivories, before the earliest known Ionian documents, belonging almost to the beginnings of Ionian culture, as usually dated, and find these much more strongly Oriental than the next set of documents available, the Ephesian.    It might be pleaded that the Orientalism of the Nimrûd ivories resulted from their being the product of Ionians domiciled in Assyria, or of Ionians supplying an Oriental market.    But that is to degrade Ionian art-work in its early stages to a low level of eclectic imitativeness, which hardly prepares us for the subsequent rapidity of its progress.    It would be more natural to draw another inference ; namely, that Ionian civilization in its beginning came under very strong and direct Oriental influences, and that its subsequent history was one of gradual emancipation from that Orientalism.    A plausible theory enough, presenting, however, certain difficulties.    How shall we account for such very strong and direct influences of the East thus early on the Ionian coast ?    How shall we explain the technical skill displayed so early by Ionians ?    How were either Ionian craftsmen or Ionian handiwork conveyed so early to the Tigris ?    There are obvious considerations which lessen these difficulties.    The antecedent existence of Aegean art, for example, and its intimate relations with the East might account for much.    But, for myself, I confess that a prior difficulty stands in the way of my acceptance of Mr. Cecil Smith's proposal.    The Nimrûd ivories are, to my thinking, altogether too Oriental in subject and style to have proceeded from any art with as much of the European spirit as even the Aegean had, still more the Ionian.    I am convinced that further research on inland north Syrian sites will produce parallels to them, and that they will soon be recognized as the work of southern Hittite craftsmen.    I do not say this without having positive reason ; but, for the present, I am not permitted to quote the evidence on which I rely.

Finally, I must notice very briefly other evidence of Eastern influence offered by the Ephesian documents. There are stylistic borrowings from Egypt, but whether by direct contact or through some medium it is hard to determine. Not a single object of certainly Egyptian fabric came to light. In the company of pseudo-Egyptian trinkets, such as scarabs with garbled hieroglyphs of a class also found largely at Naukratis and in Rhodes, and in the company of obviously imitated amulets, glazed bowls showing alien variants of Egyptian decoration, and the like, occurred one or two greatly perished objects in paste, which might have been made by Egyptian hands ; for instance, an antefix in the shape of a Bes-head. But more probably even this must be relegated to the class of pseudo-Egyptian imitations. Among the pottery, only two or three sherds can be doubtfully assigned to Naukratite fabric.

Other classes in which Egyptian influence appears are very few, and in no case is the parallelism to objects, which have actually been found in Egypt, at all close. Witness, for example, certain pendants in the form of truncheons and of human legs. If the rather remote parentage of these to Nilotic pendants be admitted, it can only be with a reservation that the Ephesian examples have undergone considerable modification at non-Egyptian hands. On the other hand, in several features where Egyptian parallelism might be looked for, as e. g. in representations of sphinxes, one does not find it. On the whole it may be said emphatically that the Ephesian evidence for direct or indirect influences of Egypt exerted on Ionia is hardly worth mentioning beside that for influences of inner Asia—a conclusion whose bearing on the whole Ionian problem will be stated presently.

It is back into the *hinterland* of Asia that all the other alien vestiges at Ephesus seem to lead us. One of the novel features in the Ephesian Treasure was the repeated presence of the hawk as a religious attribute. No other bird was represented at all. The hawk appeared in the hand of a statuette, presumably of the goddess, and many times over as a pendant, as a brooch-design, as a free-standing figure, as an *applique*; but most often perched atop a long pole, erect in one case on the head of a statuette of the goddess or of a votary. The dove we know as an attribute of the Nature Goddess elsewhere, especially in Aegean art and in the archaic Cypriote. But the hawk in a similar relation has been noticed so far only on a gold plaque from Camirus in the British Museum, and in 'Hittite' sculptures of Cappadocia; while its elevation on a pole recalls certain Cappadocian bronzes, published by Chantre, and the eagle-column of Kara Kush in Commagene. The parallel of Egyptian hawk-figures is not nearly so close. The treatment of lion-figures also, not only in ivory, but as decorative motives, is distinctly Oriental. Those in particular, which appear heraldically posed on either side of a quaint wingless figure on an electrum plaque, betray, in the hugeness of their heads, the attempt to reproduce nature which characterizes the Assyrian lions, and has influenced leonine representations so far westward as central Phrygia. To the East the long-eared gryphon with frontal horn can be traced, as can also the goddess winged or grasping her swelling breasts. The glazed ware too, if the pseudo-Egyptian objects be excepted, seems in all its varieties, even when most like that found at Camirus, to resemble the glazed clays of Babylonia more closely than the glazed pastes of the Nile. Finally let me point out that the nearest affinities in form or ornament to the Ephesian objects, whether in electrum, silver, or bronze, are presented by two groups of metal objects, found previously in inland Asia Minor. These are a small hoard of gold trinkets unearthed some twenty-five years ago in the Maeander valley near Tralles, and now in the Louvre; and the contents of certain *tumuli*, excavated at Gordium, in north-eastern Phrygia, by the brothers Körte.

## LECTURE IV

### THE OVERLAND ROUTE

In the preceding lecture various items of evidence were brought together, whose cumulative testimony seems to indicate two conclusions. First, Ionian civilization was fundamentally derived from the sub-Aegean culture, revived and to some extent leavened by a mid-European element. Second, it owed much in its infant and adolescent stages to influences of inland Asia. It is necessary now to consider by what routes and through whose mediation these latter influences could have reached the coast-land of the West.

The great preponderance of Asiatic as compared with Egyptian cultural influence, in such early Ionian products as the Ephesian objects, constitutes in itself a strong argument in favour of overland routes through the Anatolian peninsula. But not, of course, a conclusive one. The antiquities of the maritime Semitic peoples of Syria show them to have been at least as much indebted to Mesopotamia as to Egypt—indeed distinctly more to the former than to the latter. Mesopotamian models may, therefore, have, been brought also by Semites oversea. But, even if in a minority, borrowings from Egypt are so marked a feature of Phoenician culture, that one would naturally expect much more evidence of their secondary effect on Ionia than the local Ionian remains attest, had the Phoenicians been the main transmitters of Oriental models.

In any case, there were overland ways open and in active use during the required period. What were these ways ? Nature has laid down three main routes, and three only, from central Asia Minor to the western coast ; and so well has she marked these that traffic has been fain to follow them so far back as human memory runs, and follows them at this day. Enumerated from north to south they are these. First, that which follows the Sangarius valley from the neighbourhood of Angora towards the north-west angle of the peninsular coast.  Second, that of the Hermus valley, leading from the neighbourhood of Afium Kara Hissar to the sea at a point on the coast between the islands of Chios and Mitylene.  Third, one which starts from the neighbourhood of Konia, drops into the Lycus valley, and thence by way of the lower Maeander attains the sea just south of the island of Samos.  These three roads are linked one to another by a diagonal route which runs from Iconium north-westwards, through Afium Kara Hissar, and down a tributary of the Sangarius, the modern Porsuk River.  The northernmost and southernmost of the three main roads, if produced eastwards, will turn the flanks of the central salt steppe and run on over the upland of Cappadocia. Thence by easy gradients and fairly open passes both the Syrian and Mesopotamian areas, and also the Armenian and Iranian, can be reached.

Scattered about the heads of all these three main ways over a broad belt, through which lies every possible line of their continuation into the inner continent, are found the striking remains of that newly recognized inland society of the Hatti, which Greek tradition knew dimly as ' White Syrian', and scholars have hitherto called Syro-Cappadocian or Hittite.  About a third of the way down the northernmost of the three roads, and touching both the head of the second road and the diagonal connecting route, lies the district famous for the rock-monuments of the Phrygian society.  Athwart the lower part of the second and third roads—the two which, be it noted, alone debouch in Ionia—was seated the Lydian society.  These three societies, linked one to another by through routes, and all to Mesopotamia on the one hand, and to the Aegean world on the other, by continuations of those routes, have to be considered in relation to Ionia.

One only was in direct geographical contact with Mesopotamia, namely, the first-named.  This society is shown, by its monuments, to have had certainly the most extensive power, and to have been earliest in date.  If there were an

overland chain of communication between Mesopotamia
and Ionia, the Hatti must have furnished the easternmost
link. Not suspected by modern scholars till less than
forty years ago, then recognized for a while in Syria only,
and not till lately acknowledged to have been at least
as much Anatolian as Syrian, the 'Hittite' civilization is
found by almost every successive explorer of Asia Minor
to have had a wider area than his predecessors imagined,
and to have more thoroughly filled its area. It is now a
wholly obsolete view that the Anatolian 'Hittite' monuments are but strayed memorials of raiding parties from
a Syrian capital. Hardly less obsolete is the belief that
they mark the mere passing presence of warriors and
merchants circling around two or three Cappadocian centres,
whether these were Syrian colonies or not. The latest
discoveries of Sir William Ramsay and Miss Gertrude Bell
in the Lycaonian and south Phrygian regions, and of the
Liverpool and Cornell Expeditions in southern Cappadocia, added to data collected by officials of the Constantinople Museum, make it perfectly clear that 'Hittite'
civilization was at home over all central and eastern Asia
Minor during a certain period. It sat right astride of all
routes from the Aegean Sea to inner Asia, and for that
matter, since it also occupied all fertile land in north Syria,
of all eastward continental routes whatsoever from the
Mediterranean. Wherever and whenever deep excavations
come to be undertaken hereafter over the immense area
between the head-waters of the Syrian Orontes and those
of the Anatolian Sangarius, and between Mesopotamia and
the western edge of the Anatolian plateau, a 'Hittite'
stratum will be looked for, and seldom in vain.

Two conclusions have long been accepted about these
remains. First, that the period, of which they are memorials, comes down as late at least as the end of the eighth
century, and ascends thence to a remote antiquity, whereto
no superior limit can be fixed later than 2000 B.C. Second,
that the civilization, represented by those monuments, fell,
in its later period, under strong Mesopotamian influence.

Indeed, with the expansion of the Assyrian monarchy, it can almost be said to have been absorbed by Mesopotamian culture. These two conclusions are very important to our present purpose. If there existed all over central Asia Minor, down to the opening of the archaic Hellenic period, a civilization permeated by Mesopotamian influences, the first and most vital link in the required overland chain between the Tigris and Ionia may be considered established.

Both these conclusions have been powerfully supported by the remarkable results of the only extensive scientific excavation yet undertaken in inner Asia Minor, that now in progress under the auspices of the Berlin Archaeological and Nearer Asia Societies at Boghazkeui in north-western Cappadocia. Here Drs. Winckler and Puchstein, with assistants, are exploring the large city whose existence, ruins, and singular rock-sculptures were made known to scholars by Texier and Hamilton more than seventy years ago, and first scientifically surveyed by MM. Perrot and Guillaume in the sixties. But the earliest recognition of them for ' Hittite ' is to be credited to Sayce. Situated not far east of Angora, but beyond the Halys, this strong place lies on the natural eastward continuation of the northern continental road. On that account and because of the obvious importance of its remains, it has generally been guessed to be the Pterium or Pteria, which, according to Herodotus, King Croesus captured on his march beyond the Halys. But that identification remains a guess, in no way confirmed as yet by the excavations. Latterly the Pterian name has been claimed for an early site discovered at Ak-alan, in the lowest part of the Halys basin, which more nearly fulfils the indication given by Herodotus, that Pteria was κατὰ Σινώπην πόλιν τὴν ἐν Εὐξείνῳ πόντῳ μάλιστά κη κειμένη.

The results of Winckler's excavation, so far as it has gone, have yet to be published in any but the most summary form. Almost the only discovery, about which we have been informed in detail, is that of *disiecta membra* of archives, written on clay tablets in cuneiform script and in two languages, the one Babylonian, the other presumably the local tongue. Not only do the script of all, and the language of some of these documents proclaim that the Cappadocian, or Hatti, and the Mesopotamian civilizations were in close connexion, but the contents of some of the tablets, which are couched in the Babylonian language, speak to very intimate political relations. The Kings of the Hatti from Subbiluliuma to that monarch, whom Rameses II called Khetasar, seem to have kept Babylon informed of their wars and treaties, and the last-named king wrote to the Babylonian Court, after Katashmanturgu's death, a letter which argues that the two Powers had common friends and common fears. In Subbiluliuma's time, the opening of the fourteenth century B. C., the Hatti of Cappadocia (though not for the first time) appear to have swept in force into Syria, overcome the Mitanni on the middle Euphrates, and established themselves at Carchemish. Thenceforward geographical position and trade kept them in the closest touch with Mesopotamia, and they felt the earliest effects of the rise of the new north Semitic power on the Tigris. From the reign of Tiglath Pileser I (1100 B.C.), at any rate, the Hatti were in constant relations, hostile or neutral, with the Ninevites, and thenceforward their art shows such marked Assyrian characteristics that it hardly retains its individuality. Both at that epoch, which falls very near the traditional date of Ionian beginnings, and previously, Mesopotamian influences evidently had easy passage on to the Anatolian plateau. The confirmation of this fact by Winckler's discoveries is what most concerns our present purpose, among all the remarkable results of his excavation of Boghazkeui.

That the Hatti monarchy, however, could ever have come into direct contact with infant Ionia there is no reason to suppose. The period at which it seems possible that it extended its political might to the Aegean, and left as memorials the rock figures of Nymphi, must be placed much earlier than the usual date assigned to Ionian colonization. I take it to be highly probable that that period coincided with the earlier part of the Late Minoan Age, and not less probable that the Hatti realm was that inland continental Power which, as I have assumed, kept Aegean settlers off the Anatolian coasts. I said in an earlier connexion that this assumption would gain much in probability if it could be shown that a strong inland Anatolian Power did actually decay about the period usually assigned to the colonial expansion of Hellas. Let us look to the annals of that northern Mesopotamian Power, whose rise to supremacy in the old Babylonian area was foreseen and dreaded by the king of the Hatti, if we may judge by one of the newly-found letters addressed to the Court of Babylon. A large part of the known history of Assyria consists in records of recurrent attacks on these Hatti and neighbouring peoples. These ended in the complete subjection of the Syrian part of the Hatti realm, about the close of the eighth century B.C., when Carchemish and its king were captured by Sargon III, and the latter raided into Asia Minor. But we can also trace earlier Assyrian marches and annexations far beyond Taurus. There can be little doubt that not only the Syrian but the Cappadocian province suffered a long series of disastrous shocks, resulting in repeated amputations, during the centuries at the close of the second and the opening of the first millennia before our era. If Cappadocia was not denuded of all the southern part of its Federation or Empire, and did not itself become tributary to Assyria till after 1000 B.C., it had demonstrably been weakened sufficiently long before to account satisfactorily for the withdrawal of its political influence from the Aegean shores. The Nymphi figures were left high and dry by an ever-receding tide, and the long-pent forces of the western isles and Aegean coasts found opportunity at last to flow eastward.

It was apparently out of this ruin of Hatti power that two Anatolian monarchies rose successively into the view of history in Western regions, which probably had been previously subject to Cappadocia. Of these, that which seems to have attained earliest to a position conspicuous from afar was the Phrygian.  The Assyrians did not come to knowledge of it till they had broken down the Hatti barrier.  In their inscriptions they make no allusion to Phrygia till nearly the close of the eighth century, when it appears as the land of the Muski with a king Mita, i.e. Midas. But to the West it was probably known much earlier.  As Professor W. M. Ramsay said just twenty years ago, in the masterly study of Phrygian art which he contributed to the *Journal of Hellenic Studies*, its kings, prior to the establishment of the Mermnad dynasty in Lydia, ' bulked more impressively in the Greek mind than any other non-Greek monarchy :  their language was the original language and the speech of the Goddess herself ; their country was the land of  great fortified cities, and their kings were the associates of the gods themselves.'  Nor was it only from afar that the Greeks of Asia heard of Phrygian royalty.  We are told that a princess of Cyme was wedded by a Phrygian king in the eighth century, and that at least one prince of the Midas name sent offerings to the Delphic shrine. Interposed between the Asiatic Greeks and the home of the old Hatti society, the Phrygian state seems to have concealed the latter almost entirely from Greek view until its own collapse at the hands of the Cimmerian hordes ; and not till it related the expedition of the last king of semi-Hellenized Lydia beyond the Halys, did Greek literature make its solitary reference to the long moribund empire of Cappadocia.

The impression made by Phrygian power on the Greek mind is fully justified by the material remains which the former has left to our day.  Even Boghazkeui cannot show such a wonderful group of rock monuments as distinguishes that hilly district between Afium Kara Hissar and ancient Dorylaeum, which commanded both the Sangarius and Hermus roads to the sea.  The huge scarp, carved with geometric maeanders in imitation of a curtain, hung below a decorated pediment which is inscribed in a Greek-seeming alphabet with the style and titles of one of the Midaean monarchs, remains the grandest of Anatolian tombs ;

and there are above a score other sepulchral façades, not far away, almost worthy to be compared with it.   The Acropolis above the beetling crags about the Midas Tomb has a fortified summit nearly half a mile in length ;   and, in all likelihood a large lower town, which waits the explorer's spade, spread about its base.   There is no region of ancient monuments which would be better worth examination, both above and below ground, than this home of the Phrygian power ;   none that can be recommended more strongly to a Western nation prepared to spend a few years and some thousands of pounds in elucidating the origins of Greek civilization.   Several other neighbouring cities offer hardly less tempting remains, notably that to which pertained the rock tombs of Ayazinn with their famous reliefs of lions and panoplied warriors, and that other on and about the dizzy acropolis of Kumbet.   In no case is there great depth of overlying deposit, or much cumber of later remains. All the sites lie in a fair, cool upland district amid pine woods and beside running waters, and are tenanted by a sturdy, pastoral peasant folk.   Phrygia is a veritable digger's paradise.

It was made clear long ago by Perrot and Ramsay that the Phrygian homeland was once pervaded by strong Syro-Cappadocian influence.   There is at least one rock monument bearing Hittite hieroglyphs at the Midas City itself ; and a fragment of a stone, similarly inscribed, was dug out of a tumulus near Beykeui, a few miles away.   On the east the sculptures of Giaur Kalessi in Galatia link these Hittite monuments to these of north Cappadocia ;  and on the west, the Nymphi figures, so remarkably like those of Giaur Kalessi in pose and character, continue the series to within sight of the Aegean Sea.   Although, for lack of excavation we have, so far, practically nothing whereby to judge the earlier Phrygian civilization, except rock monuments, there are enough features in these to refer their artistic origin eastward even to Mesopotamia.   To take but one example.   Mesopotamian is the general treatment of the ubiquitous lion with his heavy square head and conven-

tionalized hair and externally shown muscles, who is often
posed erect in the familiar heraldic opposition of the Orient.
That before the epoch of great Phrygian kings, whose fame
reached the early Asiatic Greeks, Phrygia was politically
dependent on Cappadocia and under the influence of its
civilization, hardly admits of question.   Therefore, it is
scarcely less certain that those influences of Mesopotamia,
which were early and increasingly felt in Cappadocian
civilization, must have had free play down, at any rate, to
the western edge of the plateau of Asia Minor.

There has, however, been noted in the Phrygian monumental remains another cultural element, which seems not
Cappadocian.  This has been generally connected with
a different racial stock, which later Greek tradition regarded
as the typical Phrygian, and derived from quite another
source, namely, south-eastern Europe.  I need not recapitulate the familiar literary and mythological evidence,
which has caused the identity of the Thraco-Briges with
one element in the Phrygian society to be accepted.  There
is every reason to accept it, and to believe that in the
period of Hatti decline on the one hand, and of Aegean
eclipse on the other, tribal movements did take place
across the Hellespont, some echo of which probably yet
resounds in the songs of the War of Troy.  That story was
to repeat itself a little less than a thousand years later,
when Kelts from Illyria would sweep through the broken
Macedonian kingdoms to make in northern Phrygia the
Galatia of Roman history.  It is by those same movements,
without doubt, that we must explain the traces of Phrygian
societies on the Aegean shores which are preserved for us in
cult-legends of Mount Ida ;  in traditions of a Phrygian
Troad ;  in the localization of Greek Pelopid myths about
Smyrna, and, probably, in the actual survival there of certain
early monuments already referred to, namely the Tantalus
group.

I need not dwell on this European element in Phrygian
civilization, since my present theme is the transmission of
Mesopotamian influences.  And it is the less necessary

to do so because the monumental evidence for its presence
is, for the most part, of comparatively late date, and
probably posterior to the Ionian Migration. But, for a
certain reason, it is not without an indirect bearing on our
problem. It was probably responsible for those features in
the later Phrygian monuments which are so closely parallel
to features of the Ionian and Carian remains that they tell
strongly in favour of early intercourse between the west
coast and the interior. Such, for example, are the alphabetic
script with which several of the Sangarius monuments and
some Cappadocian ones are inscribed ; the armament of
crested helmet and round targe borne by warriors on a
certain Phrygian relief ; and the pediments and mouldings
seen on many Phrygian facades. These features are so
Greek in appearance that they have been almost universally
assumed to be derived from Ionia. That, however, is not
so necessarily their true history as has been supposed.
They all make an earlier appearance on monuments in
Phrygia than in western Anatolia. Even in the case of
the Phrygian alphabet, if we ascribe its forms and values to
Ionia, we are presuming their use there at a remoter age than
one of which we have any memorials. And if the Phoenician
alphabet is no longer to be regarded as the sole parent
of the Ionian, the arguments by which Ramsay supported
both his theories of the derivation of the Phrygian system,
whether from Cyme or from Sinope, cease to be cogent.
Some form of linear signary is proved by the incised potsherds found at Tordos in Transylvania to have been in use
in neolithic south-eastern Europe ; and the famous
inscription of Lemnos, which is in a character like the
Phrygian, though not in the Phrygian language, occurred,
it must be remembered, geographically on the possible
route of passage. One cannot help suspecting that the
derivation of the Phrygian alphabet from the Greek has
been over easily accepted, and that the former may have
been rather an independent selection from that large body
of linear symbols which seem to have been in use from very
early times among different and widely distributed sections

of the dark ' Mediterranean Race ' in the Aegean, west
Asiatic, and south-east European areas.   If that be the
true history of the Phrygian writing system, it may very
well have been the parent rather than the child of the
Asiatic Greek alphabet.

For my present purpose, however, the mere fact that these
parallel features exist is alone of importance.   It is difficult
to suppose them all of independent origin in each of the
two civilizations ; and if not independent, they equally
prove the passage of influence along the inland ways of
Asia Minor, whether they originated in the West or in the
East.   But of course they are of more support to my general
argument if they were present in Phrygia before they
appeared in Ionia.   For in that case, they add their testimony
to the rest which speaks to a flow of influence from the interior
to the western coast in the early Ionian period.   I will
therefore venture to say in conclusion that the balance
of evidence is distinctly more in favour of Phrygian influence
upon early Ionian society than of early Ionian influence
on Phrygian society.   In the history of the latter it is long
before we can detect any certain traces of Hellenic influence.
While the Lydians were armed as Greeks in the army of
Xerxes the Phrygians retained their Cappadocian equipment.   The Phrygian language persisted in local use down
to the Christian era.

Such connexion as there was between Phrygia and early
Ionia probably was conducted in the main not by direct
communication but through yet another link in the inland
chain, that Lydian society through whose territory ran
for a long distance the two routes leading from the interior
to Ionia.   Concerning Lydia our knowledge is at once
greater and less than concerning any other non-Greek
society of Asia Minor.   On the one hand the literary traditions and even the historical facts, recorded about early
Lydia by Greeks, are far fuller and more informing than
about either Phrygia or Cappadocia.   On the other, the
material evidence from Lydian soil is much more scant in
quantity and poor in quality.   Both classes of evidence

remain very nearly as they were more than a quarter of a century ago, when Radet had just published his monumental monograph on the Mermnad dynasty, and the prophetic audacity of Sayce had put forth the series of conjectures which make up the Lydian chapter of his *Early Empires of the East.* When the latter startled historians by boldly declaring that Lydia had once been a ' Hittite satrapy ', he relied in the first place on the Syro-Cappadocian character which he claimed for the rock-sculptures of the Kara Bel near Nymphi, and for the ' Niobe ' near Magnesia : in the second place on an interpretation of certain data recorded by Greeks concerning the pre-Mermnad dynasties. One of these, the Heraclid, opens with two Mesopotamian names, Belus and Ninus, and has for its eponymous hero the god whom Sayce identifies with the Oriental Sandan. His was a hazardous guess at that time. But whatever new light has been shed on inner Asia Minor since has served rather to support, than refute it. Our estimate of Hatti power, at any rate in the fifteenth and fourteenth centuries B.C., has been growing all the time. Since Winckler has discovered that a Cappadocian king could venture to admonish Katashmanturgu's heir in Babylon, it no longer appears in any way fantastic to believe that a Cappadocian empire may have reached at one time to the Aegean Sea ; and it may well be that the rock monuments near Smyrna, which are accompanied by ' Hittite ' hieroglyphs, are memorials neither of an independent local society nor of a mere Cappadocian raid, but of a definite political occupation by the power of the Hatti.

Mesopotamian influence, then, must have been free to flow onwards at some period from Cappadocia and from Phrygia down the valleys of the Hermus and Maeander. But alas ! there has been hardly any effort made to find whether traces of its passage exist or not, or indeed to learn anything at all by excavation in the teeming Lydian soil. The surface of the country has not been neglected. The careful journeys made by Buresch across and across it went far to determine what may and may not be found above Lydian ground. But he travelled before things Aegean, Syro-Cappadocian, or early Ionian were as well known and distinguished as now, and he died leaving his work incomplete, and rough notes for others to edit. Nor did he go far off beaten tracks. Much of Lydia is mountain, which brigands for two generations past have chosen as their peculiar haunt. Mention the Boz Dagh, the ancient Tmolus, in the hearing of any Smyrniote, and he will tell you how little is known of its recesses, and how Europeans fear to penetrate them. Rumours have reached scholars of more than one rock-sculpture in that *massif*—one was reported to Sayce by Spiegelthal as long ago as 1870—but no one has cared to verify the reports. There is a reputation still to be made by an archaeological surveyor who limits himself to no more than the *vilayet* of Aidin.

Even more virgin is the field for the archaeological digger. There has been practically no excavation at all in central-western Anatolia outside the Ionian cities. The great and famous site of Sardes, with its extraordinarily long and varied historical record, has scarcely been probed. Many explorers from Schliemann onwards have desired it, but all have shrunk from the cost and labour which its deep silt and overlying late strata would involve. Those who have made attempts on its grave-field, now called Bin Tepé, The Thousand Mounds, and on the great tumulus supposed to be that Tomb of Alyattes, which was described by Herodotus, have met with little reward. They have either found nothing except what earlier robbers had left, or nothing at all for want of perseverance. There are, however, two fragments of relief and some mottled vases and fragments from this great cemetery now in the British Museum, of which the latter are interesting on account of a wavy decoration, distantly recalling the mottled Vasiliké ware of Minoan Crete. An American syndicate now proposes to attack once more the well-known Temple site, where stand two columns of Hellenistic period. If it can carry out its project, it will assuredly open up the pre-Greek stratum, of which a section has been exposed already by natural denudation at a not distant point. It is to be hoped that its success may be great enough there to induce it to dig all the site. The old citadel, now weathered to a razor edge, is hopeless ground in itself; but much must have been washed down from it into the *talus* all round the foot. No excavation in Mediterranean lands is more devoutly to be desired than that of this great Lydian city, which must have acted as the main ultimate link between Ionia and the East.

With the exception of a little rummaging in the later city of Tralles there is no other excavation to record. The net result is that we have almost no material documents whatever of a society which, the early Greeks commonly believed, had taught them many of the higher arts of life. Not a single document, for example, has been found in Lydia which can be used to illustrate the writing inscribed, according to Herodotus, on pillars over the Tomb of Alyattes, or to give us further knowledge of the local speech, extinct at the Christian era, whereof a few words, all seemingly Indo-European, have been preserved to us by grammarians. An illegible stone found near Thyatira and since lost, and a doubtful fragment of scratched stone, bought in Smyrna and now at Oxford, claim alone to represent Lydian written documents found in Lydia. From alien lands there is one rude *graffito*, cut by some foreign labourer in the sandstone quarries of Silsileh on the Nile, which has been proposed for Lydian by its finder, Sayce, on the strength of two of the names it contains. Of the gold work of this country, whose riches, from the time of Gyges to that of Croesus, were a proverb in Greek mouths and are a proverb still, we have only a fair number of electrum coins and two groups of trinkets. One is of very rude type, found, perhaps, at Sardes in 1898; the other, already alluded to in the preceding lecture, is in more developed style, and was found near Tralles nearly thirty years ago, and doubtfully called Lydian. A few small bronze objects in Western museums have been reported as found in Lydia; but their provenience is doubtful and their importance is, in any case, trivial.

This lack of archaeological evidence is only redeemed, to
a certain degree, by the literary traditions of the Greeks.
These, however, make it abundantly clear, in any case,
that the relations between the coastal cities and Lydia must
have been very intimate in the archaic Ionian period, and
that Lydia seemed to Ionia to possess the older culture.
The latter evidently held the former to have been the main
trading Power of the West Asiatic world—' le grand inter-
médiaire ' in Radet's phrase.  The belief of Herodotus,
himself an Asiatic Greek, that the Lydians first used coined
money in precious metals and were the first retail-traders
(κάπηλοι), cannot be too much insisted upon.  For,
taken together, these statements can only mean that, in
Ionian opinion, it was chiefly Lydians who had traded with
the Greek cities in their early days.  So significant indeed
is Herodotus's statement that it seems to have troubled even
one who rated Lydian influence as high as Radet did.  He
tried to minimize it by suggesting that by κάπηλοι Herodotus meant merely inn-keepers.  But the word κάπηλος
never means, in Greek, what we understand in the West
by an inn-keeper, or even a publican, but rather always a
general store-keeper, like the proprietor of a Greek *bokàl*
at this day.  Such a man trades in all sorts of comestibles,
hardware, and the like, as well as in liquors, but does not
proffer lodging to travellers.

Herodotus's earlier statement that Lydians and Greeks
had similar customs, except in one peculiarly Asiatic
respect, must, perhaps, be heavily discounted by allowance
for the reflex influence of Ionia, which, prior to the historian's
day, had long been penetrating Lydia.  But other statements
made by him and by other Greek authorities show it to
have been common belief that early Greece owed to Lydia
most of its knowledge of luxuries.  Herodotus records too,
without comment, that Lydians claimed to have taught
the Greeks many of their games.  Games do not occupy a
society until it has attained to some leisure and super-
fluity.  When one civilization stands to another as its
teacher in luxuries and sports, there is no doubt which of

the two is regarded by the other as the older and more advanced.

We may safely assume then that there was a comparatively highly cultivated society in the upper Lydian valleys before there was one in the coastal cities.  Lydia probably was, when as yet Asiatic Greece was not.  You will recall that remarkable Herodotean story of Tyrsenus, who ' in the reign of Atys, son of Manes ' (Phrygian names both), led half the Lydian folk down to the bay of Smyrna, and there built ships, wherein he sailed away to found a colony in Umbrian Italy.  In the belief of those who told that story, there can hardly have been an Aeolic or Ionian Smyrna existent on the bay in the reign of this Atys, though there was already an inland monarchy able to penetrate to the coasts.  The story seems to indicate just such a state of things, as we have conjectured, probably once prevailed on the Anatolian shores.  There was some inland Power yet strong enough to keep Western settlers in the offing.  At that epoch Lydia was probably still under Hatti rule, or rather, as the royal names in the story suggest, under Phrygian clients of that power.  We know from other sources that there were close relations between Lydia and Phrygia under pre-Mermnad princes of the former country.  The fact is implied, not only by the eponymic of the legendary Atyads, but by the story of Adrastus, son of Gordius, son of Midas, who came as a suppliant to King Croesus, ἀνδρῶν φίλων ἔκγονος ἐών.  And cultural influence of Phrygia is illustrated by the oldest Lydian coins, the lion-head types upon which cannot fail to remind of the rock-sculptures of the Sangarius basin.

There is good reason to think that this influence amounted to Phrygian political dominance over Lydia in pre-Mermnad times.  Yet Lydia herself had earlier kings.  As is well-known, her dynastic history, as handed down to us by the Greeks, does not begin with the Mermnadae.  Herodotus allows for no less than twenty-two generations of a previous dynasty, the Heraclid, and for even an earlier dynasty still, and the historical character of certain of these predecessors of the Mermnadae has been conclusively demonstrated by Gelzer. But the coincidence of the great increase in Lydian power, ascribed to the efforts of the earliest Mermnadae, with the final collapse of the Phrygian monarchy under the pressure of a Cimmerian invasion points almost certainly to the latter fact having been at least partial cause of the former. There can be little doubt the Mermnadae were, in fact, the first independent monarchs of Lydia. Earlier kings had been but vassals and clients of Powers lying further inland. When ' Guggu, King of Luddi ', first of the Mermnads, applied for help to Assurbanipal, the Great King recorded in his annals that the request came from a people of which neither he nor his ancestors had previously heard. For theretofore Lydians had been confounded in Assyrian view with first one Suzerain Power, and then another, lying nearer than they to the Tigris.

By this chain of inland societies it is clear that the Asiatic and ultimately the Mesopotamian influences, which we can trace in early Ionian products, may quite well have come down to the west Anatolian coast. The eastern centre of Asia Minor was for long dominated by a Power only less Mesopotamian than Mesopotamia itself,—a Power which seems to have extended its political influence at one time even to the Aegean Sea. If that time was anterior to the Greek colonization, this Power continued, none the less, to exist inland long after the colonists had established themselves, and probably for part of the time it still dominated client states lying between its own centre and the coast. Even when these states had shaken off its overlordship, they could not rid themselves at once of prepossessions created by its long predominance. The relations of Gyges and Assurbanipal show that Lydians at least had not yet ceased to look to the Tigris in the seventh century.

For want of excavation in inland Asia Minor, however, for want of *Kleinfunde* from the Syro-Cappadocian and Phrygian areas, for want of practically any material documents of Lydia whatever, we can trace but very imperfectly this Mesopotamian influence *en route*, and hardly may do more than show that some influence did pass westward by the overland ways. It remains now to inquire whether similar influence can have passed also by the alternative way of the sea, and reached Ionia through other mediation than the Anatolian ; and, if so, what share of responsibility other middlemen must take for the total element of the Orient in early Ionian civilization. This inquiry involves a discussion of the westward expansion of the Syrian Semites, and in particular of the Phoenicians.

# LECTURE V

## THE LEVANT ROUTE

HITHERTO I have failed to make much use of those earliest literary documents of archaic Greece, the Homeric Epics. The reason is simple. They, for their part, fail to throw much light on any part of Asia, inland or littoral, beyond the small district in which the Trojan War was waged. Homer may have begged his bread through cities of Ionia, which would claim him dead; but in spite of these peregrinations (possibly because of them!) he has given posterity much less information about what lay east of the Aegean Sea than about what lay west thereof. We learn features of one or two Anatolian districts, such as the Caystrian Plain. But Lydians are never mentioned, though there is reference to Maeonians living under Tmolus. Phrygians march with the Trojan realm on the east and their land is vaguely εὐτείχητος, a land of fenced cities; but nothing is said from which their true position in Anatolian society could be inferred. To the Hatti realm there is no allusion whatever, nor any to Mesopotamian Powers. Why, after all, should Homer have alluded to these? There were, of course, far greater monarchs in Homer's time and world than Agamemnon, and Powers far more powerful than Troy or Sparta or Mycenae : but the bard was not concerned with them. He had to sing but the fortunes of a fleet of Achaean sea-rovers, who swooped from the west upon a corner of a strange coast, and were joined by a few others from Aegean isles. The Achaeans landed, fought, raided, sacked, sailed away, and had no more to do with Asia Minor. Probably Homer could have told us next to nothing about the inner peninsula, had it been his business to do so. In any case, it was not his business. Therefore let no argument be based on his silence in this matter.

He does mention rather often, however, the people of a certain Asiatic city not in Asia Minor, namely Sidon ; and in his earliest reference (*Il.* vi. 290) speaks of Sidonians alone without other Phoenicians.   These aliens are alluded to as notable sea-rovers and purveyors of choice goods ; but no individual of the race actually appears among the *dramatis personae* of the Epics, and only one, a certain Phaedimus of Sidon, is named.   When the poet has occasion to speak of a work of fine art, he usually ascribes its fabrication to a Greek god—in one case even when it is found in a Phoenician hand.   But if to a mortal, then sometimes to a Sidonian.   In alluding to the delicate art of tinting ivory, he gives us to understand that this was peculiar to certain peoples of Asia Minor, the Maeonians and Carians : and there is a great deal of artistic work described in the Epics, especially in the Odyssey—that in the Spartan and Phaeacian palaces for example—which the poet evidently understood to be of local fabric.   Indeed, a greater part in Homeric society is often assigned to the Sidonians by modern scholars than Homer himself has assigned them.   As Professor J. L. Myres pointed out some years ago, by far the most of the navigation alluded to in the Epics is carried on by Greeks in Greek ships—a fact to be borne in mind by all who are fascinated by M. Victor Bérard's *Les Phéniciens et l'Odyssée*.   What legitimately we may gather from the Homeric poems on the matter amounts to this.   The society which produced these poems (and probably also the heroes of them) was more accustomed to the visits of Sidonian ships than to those of any other alien craft, and Sidonian ships brought to it some of the foreign products which it was wont to use.   The Achaean society itself, however, was one of sea-roving and warlike adventurers, and very far from inartistic or unproductive.   When its poets ascribe its superfine works of art to the hands of its gods, we have no more right to assume they believed those works foreign, than that the saga writers of northern Europe regarded all the magic swords of Norse, German, or Danish heroes as strange products of alien races. As the great man of a heroic age may become a demigod even in his lifetime, so a great work of primitive art may be ascribed to godlike hands, even by a generation which could remember the actual fabricator.

The Homeric evidence, however, would alone justify us in conceding to the Phoenicians some part in the moulding of early Hellenic culture. Their cargoes of fine objects of art may have consisted largely of the productions of others ; while the residue, if we may judge by what we know of actual Phoenician *Realien*, was almost certainly of a derivative and unspontaneous character. But through Phoenician mediation much must have reached the shores of Greece which could not have been without inspiriting effect on a society which, presumably, was just beginning, under the influence of the Achaean blood, to renew its old Aegean vigour, and resuscitate artistic instincts. And the Homeric is, of course, not the only evidence in their favour. Both Herodotus and Thucydides, among the earlier Greek historians, confirm the fact of Phoenician visits to prehistoric European Greece and the influence there of Phoenician trade. Philology, claiming Semitic derivation for a number of early place-names round the Greek coasts, has suggested that this trade entailed the establishment of factories and settlements : but not only is Homer silent about these, but excavators have found as yet no trace of them.

Moreover, there is one other argument to be put to Phoenician credit. Even if the Cadmean legend and all its derivatives are under present suspicion of not having had any original Semitic reference at all, the Cadmean φοῖνιξ having been the ' red ' (i.e. dark) Aegean man, some Phoenician responsibility for the Greek alphabet cannot altogether be explained away. It is true that the recent discovery of an earlier script of the Greek area, some of whose later linear characters approximate closely to archaic Hellenic forms, has forced a reconsideration of the accepted theory, and will perhaps revolutionize our views as to the source from which the Phoenicians themselves derived alphabetic writing. It is true that the classical literary tradition concerning the origin of the Hellenic alphabet is not worth much ; for it is wholly expressed by authors of the Roman period, with the single exception of Herodotus, whose statement was perhaps the authority of all the others, and moreover implied not a well-known fact of the age, but a reasonable conjecture of the author's own. It is true that the variation in the alphabetic values of certain symbols in different parts of Greece, and the appearance of certain other symbols in the Hellenic system, whose forms and values are demonstrably not of Phoenician derivation, raise difficulties. It is true, finally, that a minority of the Hellenic characters bear names without meaning in any known Semitic tongue. But despite all these considerations, the double fact that the majority of the Greek alphabetic names are indeed Semitic, and that the Semitic alphabetic order is also the Hellenic order, so far as the shorter of the two alphabets goes, makes it certain that Semites, and with hardly a doubt Phoenicians, exercised some strong local influence when the Hellenic societies were first developing alphabetic writing. In communications between those societies Phoenicians must have been playing so large a part that the names, the values, and the order of their alphabetic symbols ultimately imposed themselves in a great measure all round.

It is necessary, however, to enter a strenuous protest at this stage against really good evidence for the Phoenicians having prosecuted a carrying trade in the Aegean Sea at a certain epoch, being used to argue a very much wider conclusion. The share borne by Semites in the transmission of Eastern influences to Greek coasts implies neither that they were the only transmitters, nor that they themselves were a people of such high productive capacity, that they appeared to the infant Hellenes to be a superior race and masters in civilization. These exaggerations, which colour almost all the standard accounts of early Greek history, are due to a misunderstanding of various evidence. Some of this—for example the Homeric—was always of clear enough significance if carefully analysed, while the rest could hardly be rightly appreciated till lately. Foremost stands, of course, the Aegean evidence ; but thereon I need not waste words. The day is now past when ' Mycenean ' civilization was believed to owe a heavy artistic debt to Phoenicia, and archaeologists saw Semitic handiwork in the finer objects found by Schliemann.

Another kind of evidence, however, namely the Cypriote of post-Aegean date, needs more consideration. Cyprus has often been represented as more Phoenician than Phoenicia. But what are the facts ? There was certainly a Phoenician settlement under a Phoenician dynasty at Kition, near the modern Larnaca. A comparatively large number of Phoenician inscriptions has been found there, far more indeed than in all Phoenicia itself. The *Corpus of Semitic Inscriptions* contains seventy-seven from Kition alone as against nine from the whole Syrian coast. A small number has been found also at the neighbouring Idalium, which was at one time subject to Kition. In the whole of the rest of the island not above a dozen Phoenician inscriptions in all have turned up, and these are isolated specimens ; e. g. one at Golgoi, one near Lapethus, one lately at Old Paphos and some at Chytri. The whole of these texts are of late date, none being earlier than the fifth century B. C., with the single exception of that written on the fragments of a bronze bowl, dedicated to Baal of Lebanon, and in all probability an imported object. We are told that the Persian King, Xerxes, when he occupied Cyprus in the year 479 B. C., sent to Tyre for a certain Baalmelik to found a dynasty at Kition ; and the actual Semitic remains in Cyprus do nothing to negative the contention that this was the beginning of Phoenician dominance in any part of the island whatsoever. There may have been earlier trading settlements, but there is no good evidence to prove their existence. Even the Biblical mention of *Chittim* as a dependency of Tyre must not be insisted upon, while many philologists hold that the aspirated initial of the name precludes its identification with Kition. Since the Phoenician dynasts came to an end with Alexander's conquest, we cannot credit Semitic dominance in Cyprus for more than a century and a half : and this brief period falls wholly in classical time.

Moreover, during that same period, the island remained otherwise Hellenic. Even in Idalium, under Semitic rule, inscriptions show us that the names of the leading citizens and the civic organization were Greek. Perrot had to admit this awkward fact while dealing with Cyprus as a mere artistic dependency of Phoenicia. He had also to admit certain other anti-Semitic facts about early Cyprus. First and foremost, its historic language, so far back as there are any inscriptions to witness to it, was Greek. Secondly, this language was expressed by a non-alphabetic syllabary, which is related, not to any Semitic system of writing, but to a wholly different group of scripts. Since Perrot wrote his Cypriote chapters, we have learned a good deal more about that group, and on certain clay balls found at Enkomi have now earlier Cypriote texts to study. It has become clear that there was a family relation between the primitive Cypriote writing and the linear Cretan of the Late Minoan Period, which was pre-Phoenician. The former belongs then generically to the Aegean system. Cypriote syllabic writing survived in use to a very late age, even into the third century B.C. Not till then did it give way at last to the Greek alphabetic κοινή. It has often been remarked that the syllabic system, which thus long persisted, provided an extraordinarily cumbrous means of expressing the Greek tongue ; and the inference has been rightly drawn that it must have been very firmly established in use before the far more convenient Phoenician alphabetic system was introduced into the island. The latter can hardly be believed to have ever been used by a large, much less by a dominant, element in the population.

Thirdly, the paramount Goddess of Cyprus is always called in the earlier inscriptions of the island by a Greek name, ἡ Ϝάνασσα, the Queen. The two chief seats of her local worship, Paphos and Idalium, are, as it happens, the two towns whose Greek character is most emphatically attested by records of proper names. At Paphos above a hundred inscriptions have been found in Cypriote, Greek, and Roman characters, but I believe only one in Semitic characters. At Idalium about half a dozen Phoenician inscriptions have been found, none earlier than the fourth century. None are known from Amathus, and one only comes from Golgoi. Whatever the Semitic features in the worship of the Cypriote goddess, her chief local seats evidently remained predominantly Greek to the end. Nay, more, it may fairly be questioned whether as a matter of fact, there were any certainly Semitic features in her cult. A similar Nature Goddess has now been recognized as paramount divinity throughout the Aegean world. If she was especially honoured in the western isle of Crete, in which Aegean civilization seems to have developed itself from a remote antiquity without serious modification from outside, the common views of a past generation concerning the eastern origin of the Hellenic Aphrodite everywhere, and the Cypriote Queen in particular, seem to call for radical revision. Many features of the latter's cult, for which parallels used to be sought on the Syrian coast, have earlier parallels in the western Aegean. The cult-use of *baetyls*, for instance, was old in Crete before we have any actual evidence for it on the Phoenician coast. Why, then, affiliate the sacred Paphian stone to Byblus ? The dove was a divine attribute of the Aegean Goddess alike in Mycenae and Crete, and rested in her hand or on her head and perched atop the sacred *baetyl*. What need, then, to look to Syrian Ishtar for the inspiration of the dove-bearing figurines of Idalium and Golgoi ? The orgiastic practices of the Paphian temple, such as ceremonial prostitution (for which, by the way, our only evidence is Christian), had parallels of course over all West Asia, even to Armenia and Babylon. But they can be paralleled also at Corinth and in Sicily.

If the Phoenicians exercised no influence on the language, the names or the script of Cyprus, and probably little or none on its cult, evidence can hardly be expected to show that they were responsible for much of its artistic expression. If we find, as we do, that the whole of the pottery in the Enkomi graves belongs to the same Aegean class as the Ialysus vases and the latest ' Reoccupation ' ware of Crete, having been lineally developed out of the style of the first and second Late Minoan periods ; if we find further that all Bronze Age ceramic and copper work in Cyprus is so far distinct from that of neighbouring areas, and shows such unmistakable signs of development from rude local beginnings that its native origin is unquestionable—then once and for ever we abandon Phoenician art as the main stock out of which the Cypriote has grown.   As Professor J. L. Myres put it in the *Catalogue of the Cyprus Museum*, ' the most universally characteristic types of Cypriote pottery do not reappear in Phoenicia and consequently cannot have been borrowed thence . . . In any case the evidence is strongly against any original dependence of Cypriote culture on any known Phoenician style.'   Further-more, we find clear evidence in Cyprus of transition from the Bronze Age style to that of the Early Iron Age.   The great majority of decorative elements in the latter have survived from the former to originate that local Geometric ornament which thenceforward would remain characteristic of Cyprus.

Turning to the objects of a more luxurious and exquisite sort, such, for example, as those in precious metals, in ivory and in compositions, we expect more evidence of foreign influence ; and we have found it, in fact, at Enkomi. But very little of that influence is certainly, or even pro-bably, Phoenician.   There is a good deal that is Egyptian. Not only do scarabs and other objects in paste of actual Nilotic fabric form part of the Enkomi Treasure, but the gold-work of the latter, both for some of its designs and for its use of granular *appliqué* ornament, may well be indebted to the fine work in precious metal, which was made in Egypt in the Ramesside age and earlier.   The recent discovery of a treasure of Rameses II's time at Bubastis has made it quite clear that, if the *polveriscolo* work of

Enkomi, of early Ionia, and of Etruria is to be traced any-whither, it is to the Egyptian metallurgy of the second millennium B.C.   Nor need we seek an intermediary between Cyprus and the Nile.   There is ample evidence to be deduced both from Pharaonic records and from the frequent occurrence of Cypriote pottery on Nilotic sites (e. g. such sherds were found by Petrie during his first season at Memphis), that Egypt and the nearest Mediterranean isle were in frequent and direct communication, from at least the time of Thothmes III.

There is also much Asiatic influence evident in the Enkomi Treasure, particularly in the ivories.   A commission on this particular art might be claimed for the Phoenicians, did its expression in the Enkomi objects show any of those charac-teristics which we associate with the best attested products of Phoenician art, e. g. those metal bowls with figure-decoration arranged in concentric zones and often accom-panied by Semitic inscriptions, which have been found at various points between Nineveh and Italy.   Those charac-teristics, namely certain eclectic and often misunderstood schemes and details of ornament, and unmistakable hard-ness and dryness of execution, are conspicuous by their absence from the Enkomi ivories.   Here one notes borrowed motives expressed with the same rare originality and life observed in the Cretan treatment of exotic subjects at a somewhat earlier Aegean period.   Whatever doubt there be about the exact date of the Enkomi graves, there can be none about the source of the culture which their contents represent.   That culture was essentially Aegean in origin and of local development.   It borrowed more directly from Egypt and Mesopotamia than did the Minoan culture in Crete, because it lay geographically more near to those regions.   But like the Minoan, it has transformed all borrowings in the crucible of its own genius.

From the art of the Enkomi Treasure the essential features of Cyprian products of the archaic historic period are easily derived.   It is not until we get to a period too late to affect the problem of Ionian origins that we can trace Syrian

modification of Cypriote art. Even then it seems to be only
a case of Syria paying back part of a debt incurred to Cyprus
itself in a slightly earlier age. Such, and so late, for example, is the Syrian influence in the ' Graeco-Phoenician '
stone statuary and the terra-cottas, of which many examples
are in the Cesnola collection. Indeed, Professor Myres puts
on record so strong an opinion as this, that the Phoenicians
had probably no art of their own at all when they first
appeared in Cyprus. If so, it is obviously absurd not only
to regard the Phoenicians as having formed the civilization
of early Hellenic Cyprus, but also to take Cyprian products
as exemplifying in their main characteristics Phoenician art.
What they exemplify, from the Enkomi Treasure to the
bracelet of Eteander of Paphos, is in all essentials the
local art of an Aegeo-Hellenic community, fundamentally
non-Semitic. If there was any artistic impulse conveyed
by one race to another, it was the Cypriotes who inspired the Phoenicians, not the Phoenicians the Cypriotes.
That subsequently Tyrians imported their imitative wares
into the island, which had itself done much to teach them
to be productive of works of art—such wares as the beaten
bowls of Amathus, for example—and that they exported
thence Cypriote products and influences to their western
colonies—these facts do not affect the main question.
Such importation and exportation, so far as all our material
evidence goes, fell in a much later period than that at which
Hellenic civilization was in the making.

A briefer and rather different story has to be told about
Rhodes, the second and final station claimed for Phoenician
influence in its presumed conquering course towards the
West. There, too, we have to consider the fact that, in
the Ialysus graves, the earliest local evidence bears witness
not to a Phoenician civilization but to a sub-Aegean one
in communication with Ramesside Egypt. You will remember that Ialysus, with Lindus and Camirus, appears on
the Achaean side in the Iliad—a fact which, for what it is
worth, indicates that the civilization of the island had come
from the West. When we come to the group of documents

next in point of time, the contents of certain pits and graves at Camirus, which seem to belong to the seventh century B.C., we find metal-work similar to the Ephesian and like it to be most reasonably derived from a sub-Aegean source. But we find also pottery into which a new element of figure-decoration has been introduced, and ivories and objects in composite material also inspired by some non-Aegean art. Though there is an Asiatic element, especially in the ceramic decoration, the main ultimate source of this alien influence is unquestionably Egypt. Especially in the ivories do we note strong Nilotic characteristics; and quite a considerable number of figurines, amulets, scarabs and the like composite objects, either of Egyptian workmanship or closely imitated from Egyptian models, were found on the site. Similar imitations have been found in the greatest numbers at Naukratis, in the successive excavations of that site carried out since 1884: and that fact certainly suggests that not Phoenicians so much as Graeco-Egyptians are to be held responsible for the Nilotic features in the archaic art of Rhodes and of other parts of Greece. We know that natives of south-western Asia Minor were both frequent visitors to, and residents in, the Nile valley at least as early as the accession of the Saite Pharaohs. They had a quarter and a camp at Memphis, inscribed the legs of a colossus in Nubia in a local alphabet (probably of Rhodes itself) in the seventh century, and established trading posts on the Cano-pic Nile long before Amasis confined them to Naukratis Since, moreover, at the latter place they came under the full influence of that Deltaic civilization which, as we are learning more and more every day, absorbed into it much that was Mesopotamian in origin, they can quite well have transmitted to Rhodes, Anatolia and European Greece even the Asiatic element in their archaic Hellenic art.

The effect of this anti-Semitic criticism is to reduce the part played by the Phoenicians among the Greek isles and coasts, when Hellenism was in the making, to that of mere huckstering traders, who followed sea-ways opened long ago by others. At most they established factories rather than colonies at a few points, such as Kition in Cyprus, and these on sufferance. The evidence certainly raises no sort of presumption that they could have had any share worth mentioning in teaching the Greeks to be an artistic people. Nor, if we turn to the actual remains of Phoenician art for evidence, does what we find support, either by its date or by its character, any such presumption. The knowledge which we possess of that art, as practised in the homeland of Syria or in lands undoubtedly dominated at any period by Phoenicians, such, for example, as the central littoral of North Africa, is limited to a period much later than even Homer. All Phoenician products of an earlier age have to be taken on trust, partly from the Homeric references themselves, partly from a small number of statements made by later Greek and Roman writers. Some of these are traceable to Homer himself, others to Phoenician records translated into Greek by such authors as Menander of Ephesus and Philo of Byblus. There are also certain references in Hebrew history, as given both in the Old Testament and in the works of Josephus, who, however, seems to have used largely Menander's compilation. But, when we begin to be able to study its actual documents, we find Phoenician art so entirely derivative and imitative, and, moreover, so barren of variety, that we are unable to believe that it was ever independent or progressive. Future excavations may modify this judgement by adducing early evidence, now undreamed of, from Sidon, Aradus, Tyre and the western Phoenician colonies. But time goes on, and Phoenician soil remains almost as barren as ever. True, there has been but limited facility for research. Some digging, however, has been done at Sidon and Tyre, and the surface of the country has long ago been thoroughly explored. Tunisia has been in French hands for almost a generation, but early Carthaginian art is still represented by coarse, provincial work, slavishly subservient to Egyptian influence.

In fine, we remain in no position to judge by comparative standards that art-work of the early Tyrian age which Hebrew tradition so greatly glorified. There are no

material Semitic remains to speak to the existence
of anything that can be called culture in Phoenicia until
a period when Ionian society must have already reached
an adolescent stage.   There is nothing—no monument,
no coin, nor anything else—older than the ninth century
at the very earliest.   In particular, there is no known
specimen of Phoenician writing of as early a date as 900
B. C.   I am not losing sight of the fact that both the
Egyptian and the Homeric references, as well as those in
the Old Testament, witness to the Phoenicians having been
a more or less civilized people some centuries before that.
But none of these references prove, what all the archaeological documents tend to disprove, that there was such
an independent and progressive civilization among these
Semites as was needed, if a decisive cultural effect was
to be produced on such a stock as the early Ionian.
Especially must we doubt whether the Phoenicians had
any fully developed independent system of writing before
the Ionian Migration had already taken place.

As regards Ionia the sum of the matter may be stated
thus.   The absence of Egyptian cultural influence from the
oldest products of Ephesus, the absence of actual Phoenician
fabrics both there and in Rhodes, and Greek tradition that
the Asiatic Greeks were educated in the ways of commerce
by the peoples of the inner peninsula, constitute, all taken
together, a formidable presumption that Eastern influences
reached the coast by overland routes in far greater measure
than by the sea-ways of the Levant.   But the presumption
is not final.   The door must be left open to the Semites as
possible carriers of Mesopotamian goods.   If it could be
proved that shortly before the opening of the first millennium B. C. the Phoenicians were detached from Egyptian
influence, and were acting as the carriers of little else than
Asiatic wares, their agency might still have been considerable.   And this, as it happens, is not at all an improbable
case.   It is a well-known fact that after the time of Rameses
the Third, i. e. early in the twelfth century B.C., Egyptian
records cease for a time to mention direct relations with

Asiatic peoples. We hear no more thenceforward of wars with those strong Kheta confederacies, which had been disputing Syria with the Pharaohs since the middle of the Eighteenth Dynasty. The obvious, and probably the true, explanation of this change is the rise of the Kingdom of Israel in the zone between Syria and the Nile valley. This kingdom, while it remained vigorous, acted as a buffer state. If so, then central and northern Syria must once more have fallen completely under influences of Mesopotamia, which, for that matter, had always been potent among the western Semites. For, even at the height of the Egyptian Empire in Asia, they seem never to have used the Egyptian hieroglyphic system. In Philistia we find a linear signary allied to the Aegean system, and in Phoenicia, among the educated classes, cuneiform writing. In the northern interior the Hittite hieroglyphic system was always supreme, with cuneiform as an alternative.

The products, therefore, which the coastal Semites would have been conveying westward about the date of the Ionian Migration, were most likely to have been of Mesopotamian character. The first known political contact between Phoenicia and Assyria falls as late as the ninth century in the reign of Ithobal, King of Tyre. But those ‘Assyrian cargoes’, which Herodotus says the Phoenicians began to carry soon (αὐτίκα) after their establishment on the Syrian littoral, might have come down to the west coast by caravan routes long before that. The progress of research in north Syria is revealing ever more clearly the importance of an inland civilization, geographically interposed between Phoenicia and Mesopotamia, which was in full vigour in the latter part of the second millennium B. C. To judge by its remains, great and small, it must have been exceedingly productive. This is that southern ‘Hittite’ civilization of which I have spoken already in connexion with Cappadocia. The place which, in the Assyrian records referring to the Hatti, appears always as their capital, must have been a great trade centre   We can infer as much from the simple fact that a standard of weight, the *maneh* or *mina* of Carchemish, was so named, and in common use in the populous centres of Mesopotamia. Carchemish was situated on the Euphrates itself, at a much-used crossing of the river, and according to the interpreters of Egyptian and cuneiform texts, on the right or Syrian bank. If so, there is no doubt that it is represented by the large fortified site of Jerabis, about fifteen miles down stream from Birejik. Here are to be seen a great artificial mound, overhanging the river, city walls enclosing a horseshoe, whose longest diameter is nearly half a mile, a massive cyclopean revetment to pen back the Euphrates, and four sculptured slabs of very good Hittite-Assyrian style, standing or lying in a deep trench made nearly thirty years ago at the foot of the Acropolis. Other monuments, found at the same time, were sent to the British Museum, and these testify sufficiently by their hieroglyphic inscriptions, as well as by their artistic style, to the Hittite character of the site. They remain the finest sculptures yet found in all the area of Hittite civilization, and though they display the unmistakable characteristics of Hittite art, they show also, as might be expected, very marked influence of Mesopotamia. Above the level of the Hittite city lie considerable remains of a town of the Christian time, whose identity is not certain. Its presence argues the long-continued importance of this site as commanding a crossing of the Great River.

Nor is this the only important Hittite site in Syria. Both banks of the Euphrates, during the hundred miles of its middle course, from the point where it emerges from the Taurus mountains to that where it enters the desert, show one uninterrupted series of flat-topped mounds, a fresh one rising every few miles ere sight of the last has been lost ; and in three or four of these chance has brought to light Hittite monuments. From the great earth-mound of Samosata to that crowned by the castle of Kalat en-Nejm, the whole series is Hittite. If you leave the river for central Syria, similar mounds will almost never be out of your sight on any road you choose to travel from the upper Orontes valley, where lies the site of Kadesh, about to be excavated by the French, to the Taurus at Marash. Professor von Luschan, the excavator of Sinjerli, has told me that he counted not less than six hundred in north-western Syria alone. Some of the Syrian mounds, e.g. those at Hamah, Aleppo and Tell Bashar, which have yielded Hittite remains, are even larger than that at Jerabis.

This vast group of desolate city sites, which mark the surface of north Syria and the adjacent border of Mesopotamia with a veritable eruption of earth-pimples, witnesses to the disappearance of an exceptionally well-developed society, one to which its command of the main continental routes from Egypt, from Mesopotamia and from Asia Minor, must have given great commercial and strategic importance. You need only take a passing survey of the region to understand why the Great Kings of Assyria so long and so patiently strove to possess it, and why the Hatti play so great a part in their annals.

It is imperatively necessary, if we are to understand the transmission of culture influences of Mesopotamia and especially of weight-standards to the Mediterranean peoples, to learn more about this important intermediate civilization of north Syria. Not only small antiquities, which are picked up by scores on the surface of its sites, but certain of the larger monuments still in place are of types which hitherto would have been put down at sight as Phoenician. The inland Syrian civilization, I feel no doubt, ought to be credited, and will hereafter be credited, with the fabrication of a very great deal which has been ascribed, not only in modern times but in ancient, to the coastal Semites, simply because the latter were the chief carriers of it to the West. I have already said that I believe we have actually in the British Museum a notable group of north Syrian products, in the shape of the Nimrûd ivories. On the middle Euphrates existed just such a society as could have produced them— one independent and vigorous, but for long in close touch with both the Egyptian and the Mesopotamian cultures, and probably at one time also in contact with that of the Aegean in the later Bronze Age. It is this society's direct or indirect influence, whose ultimate formative influence on Ionian art is illustrated by the Ephesian ivories.

Till this year no excavation has been carried out in inland Syria except at Sinjerli, the mound which covers the remains of the chief town of a minor kingdom, Shamal. The culture which its monuments show is of the Hatti class, but no Hittite inscriptions have come to light, and the style of the art is provincial compared to the monuments of Jerabis. During this past spring a beginning has been made by Professor J. Garstang for the University of Liverpool on another large north Syrian site, that at Sakjegözu, about a day's march east of Sinjerli. The style of the sculptures so far uncovered is superior to those found at Sinjerli, but no Hittite inscriptions have yet come to light. Much is to be hoped from the further course of these excavations ; but more will come from Jerabis or another of the larger sites in the near neighbourhood of the Euphrates itself. There lay the focus of north Syrian society. There its culture joined hands with that of Mesopotamia. There we are most likely to find the bilingual texts which will solve the still insoluble riddle of the Hittite inscriptions.

# LECTURE VI

## CONCLUSION

In this course, which I am about to conclude, I have
brought to your notice a good deal of new evidence from
very various quarters, but I do not claim to have propounded many novel conclusions. So far as I understand
their significance, the new facts concerning the origin of
Hellenic civilization tend rather to define and clear up the
truth of old theories than to suggest a fresh and revolutionary
view. Not now, or by me, is it argued for the first time that
the so-called miracle of the rise of Hellenism, early in the first
millennium B. C., is to be explained by the re-invigoration of
aboriginal societies settled for long previous ages in the
Aegean area, and possessed of an ancient tradition and
instinct of culture. Nor that this process was chiefly due
to the blood and influence of an immigrant population of less
impaired vigour, which had long been cognizant of and participant in the mid-European culture, and was itself both in
origin and development related to the elder society of the
Aegean area. Nor, again, that a secondary stimulus was
imparted to the renascence, thus initiated, by influences
of the living East, which were mainly Asiatic, and now found
renewed and better opportunities of reaching the Aegean
peoples, partly through the eastward expansion of the latter
to the shores of Asia Minor, partly through the westward
expansion of a Syrian coastal people, hitherto kept off the
seas by the Minoan navies of Crete. These views have
long been in the air. I do but offer fresh illustration of their
premisses, and seek to give definition to their conclusions.
Especially have I tried to render reasonably intelligible the
appearance of such distant influences as the Mesopotamian
in the Hellenic world. When Brunn said, in his *History of
Art,* ' der Ionische Stil gehört Niniveh, vielleicht bereits

Babylon an,' he was boldly ignoring, with the instinctive conviction of genius, the then unbridged gulf between Mesopotamia and the Aegean at the opening of the Ionian period.

In this matter of Oriental influences, as in several others, while able to adduce more probable explanations than could be offered a generation ago, I have, needless to say, left many questions open. The imperfect state in which the exploration of western Asia still remains renders it impossible to do otherwise. We are far more often in a position to show that such and such facilities favoured the passage of Eastern influences by this route or by that, than to prove by actual documents found along the suggested routes, that thus they actually did pass. The two ends of the chain are very much better known than the intermediate links. I dare not, therefore, dogmatize by which main route, that overland, or that over the Levant sea, the Asiatic influences took their way to Ionia. For the really dynamic influences of Oriental civilization the overland route is strongly favoured by the evidence ; but this does not render improbable the arrival of mere models by way of the sea through the agency of Semitic carriers.

There the question must, perforce, be left till Asiatic Turkey is opened as freely to exploration as Greece, Crete, Cyprus, and Egypt have been. In so saying I am neither oblivious nor unappreciative of the greatly increased facilities offered to explorers by the enlightened direction of the Imperial Ottoman Museum in these latter years. So far as it has lain in their power, Osman Hamdy Bey and his subordinates have encouraged research by scholars of all nationalities in Asiatic Turkey. They have, moreover, prepared a magnificent storehouse in Constantinople for the portable documents of antiquity. The hindrance has not come from those authorities. Nor, in my own experience, except in isolated cases and for temporary and often good reasons, has it come directly from any officials of the central government. But the indirect effect of a very faulty provincial administration has been prohibitive. There have been too much local insecurity too imperfect control over the ignorant and jealous populations which are now seated in many of the regions most needing exploration, and too little assurance that valuable remains of antiquity, when re-exposed, would be protected from damage or destruction. Therefore, for the archaeological digger in particular almost all the Asiatic shores of the Mediterranean, not to mention those of Turkish North Africa, still offer virgin soil. We remain deplorably ignorant even of so accessible a coast as that of western Asia Minor so far at least as those deep-lying strata are concerned which contain the documents of its earliest civilization. It is still as true as when Perrot wrote twenty years ago, that only one stratified primitive site in all Greek Asia has been explored to the bottom, namely Hissarlik.

This being the case, I proceed to advance, with all possible reserve, a summary theory of the particular circumstances which contributed to the rise of that local but most brilliant development of Hellenism, which we call Ionian civilization. The elements which went to the making of the Ionian people I take to have been essentially the same as those which went to the making of all the Hellenes whatsoever. A mass of the old Aegean stock, which had long been participant in the prehistoric civilization of the Aegean Bronze Age, came to be leavened by an infusion of northern blood drawn from the area of mid-European culture. But the proportions of the mixture were not quite the same on the Asiatic coasts as in the Peloponnesus, for instance, or in classic Crete. The Aegean element was, I conceive, relatively very much more numerous and potent in the Ionian land, although, to a very large extent, not indigenous there. Subject to the notorious risk of pressing negative evidence, especially in regard to so ill-explored an area as Ionia, I suggest that its lack of Aegean remains does exclude the central coast of Anatolia from the credit of having shared in the Aegean civilization during almost all the Bronze Age. I believe that this coast was long dominated by an inland continental Power, that of the Cappadocian Hatti, who imposed their own distinct civilization and admitted the Aegean culture only as a faint influence ascending along trade routes.

At some early epoch, however, had begun an infiltration of peoples from south-eastern Europe across the Thracian straits.   I stated in my third lecture the evidence for their appearance so far back as sub-neolithic time.   These gradually infused a European element into all the populations of the western peninsula, into the so-called Mysians, for example, into the Maeonians, into the Lydians, and into the Carians.  The European element settled in especial strength about the Gulf of Smyrna, and may very likely, as Greek tradition represented in the Pelopid myth, have subsequently re-emigrated in part to Greece.   So far, Curtius's Proto-Ionian theory is probably well founded.

An important change began to operate upon this loose tribal society towards the close of the second millennium B. C.   Owing to Assyrian pressure the dominant continental society, whose centre was in Cappadocia, shrank inwards and ceased to dominate the western coasts.   Nor did a secondary inland society, the Phrygian, which succeeded to the hege-mony on the plateau, make itself felt on the Aegean shores as the Cappadocian had done.   Much about the same time and possibly *propter hoc*, in some measure, as well as *post hoc*, the first of the northern waves which were to wash over western Greece and the isles, the Achaean, began to surge southwards.   The result was twofold.   On the one hand Achaean sea-rovers themselves made their appearance on the north-western shores of Asia Minor, overcame the local centre of Aegean power at Hissarlik, and made possible the subsequent ' Aeolic ' colonies.   On the other hand, fragments of Aegean populations were pressed out of mainland Greece and the isles by the northern invasion and began to find their way over to the shores of central and south-western Anatolia.   These brought with them that late Aegean culture of which traces have been found in Rhodes and in Caria, and these originated the Greek tradition that the latter district had been colonized by Minoan settlers

from Crete, and that ' Carians ' once held the command of
the Aegean Sea.

It is to be expected that further exploration of the
very ill-known Carian region, long rendered peculiarly
uninviting by the brigandage which followed the break-up of
the jurisdiction of the Mentesh *dere beys*, will show that this
late Minoan immigration was numerous and considerable
enough to account for those elements in cult-usages and in
nomenclature which have long been remarked as common
to historic Caria and to prehistoric Crete. Those epithets,
historic and prehistoric, I apply advisedly. All the evidence
gathered in this past decade of Aegean discovery reveals
the common elements in Crete ages before we can discern
them in Caria If the deities who bore the double-axe,
the Goddess with her Son in Crete, and Zeus Labrandeus in
Caria, are to be derived from one another, it is the latter
that is derivative. The Carian place-names ending in
*-ndus, -nda, -nthus*, and so forth, which Kretschmer holds
to be not Indo-European and to belong to the older stratum
of the population, make their appearance earlier in the
Cretan Labyrinth and in other Aegean names. The Carian
alphabet has left no epigraphic evidence of its use till well
into the first millennium B. C. ; and Mr. Evans thinks that
certain of its forms actually show derivation from the
Minoan linear script which was in use nearly a thousand
years earlier.

Upon this amalgam of Asiatic, European, and Aegean
races supervened at the last the Ionian Migration, which was
itself an amalgam. What exactly we are to understand
by that Migration, when it began and when it ended, it is
very difficult to say. Certainly it did not pass in any one
great horde. All the recorded traditions of the Hellenic
cities of Asia point to successive arrivals of comparatively
small parties, which did not always pitch at once on their
ultimate abiding-places. Migrations by sea, in the infancy
of navigation, were probably never undertaken by much
larger bodies than those which first landed in America.
Their reports, slowly filtering back, brought other parties

in their wake.  The landings in Asia probably went on for
several generations, departures being determined by events,
political and social, which took place at considerable intervals
of time on the mainland of Hellas and in the isles.  The
first departure may have been due to the Achaean influx
into Greece.  Greek tradition did, in fact, attribute the
Ionian Migration to the overcrowding of Attica with refugee
elements from the War of Troy ; and it represented it as
composed of an extraordinary number of racial elements,
among which one notes with interest Minyae of Orchomenus
whose Aegean character is unquestioned, and Cadmeians,
Pelasgi and others who were hardly less certainly part of
the older population.  Note further that the date thus
assigned by tradition, fits with the indications in Homer.
The Epics, it has often been remarked, show not only no
knowledge of a Hellenic Asia but also none of a Dorian
conquest of Peloponnesus.  They were probably anterior in
original composition to the establishment of both those
states of things.  The society they reflect is the prime of
the Achaean in its new home, and the moment probably that
of the first adventuring of the mainland peoples oversea.
Their leaders were Achaeans, but they themselves were not
all of their leaders' race.  If the Greek tradition in regard
to the remnants of the Trojan expedition, which were
collected in Attica after the war, is to be credited at all,
it certainly implies that the European forces before Troy
had been by no means purely Achaean.

In such a sense I take the Ionian Migration to be historical.
There is no reason whatever to discredit it, if it be borne
in mind that nothing is so congenial to popular tradition
as to crystallize a series of successive events into a single
one.  Thus, for example, the Dorian conquest of the
Peloponnesus was envisaged as one cataclysmic event, the
Return of the Heraclidae, although Greek literature from
Homer onwards bore unconscious witness to the fallacy.
For the Dorians had been coming south in small parties
for several generations, and were already an element in the
population of Crete when the Odyssey was composed.

It is almost always so with such migrations. Bodies of nomad Turks established themselves in Asia Minor generations before the Seljuk conquest and centuries before the appearance of the Ottomans on the stage of history. They were present in south-eastern Europe also before there was any Turkish invasion of our continent. Remember this popular tendency to foreshorten history, and you will find nothing in the tradition of an Ionian Migration but what you would expect. The narrow and lean peninsula of Greece doubtless received during many generations an intermittent overflow of vigorous tribes from the inner European lands, tempted by the prospect of plundering a rich decadent society, or pressed out of earlier homes by some *force majeure*. Considerable and successive displacements of the older southern population must have ensued. Unable to withstand the iron weapons of the invaders, the weakest aboriginals would be reduced to serfdom ; the strongest would be apt to take ship and seek new homes. Even some of the new-comers would join or follow the emigrants in search of further fortune, and would be welcomed as leaders for their natural vigour and their better craft of war. But these would be a small numerical minority. They would in all likelihood have few or no women of their own folk with them, but would take women of the older population to their beds. The consequent children would learn of their mothers rather than of their fathers ; and the type of civilization which would develop in the new country would be in the main that of the elder race.

An objector might demur at this point. What about the evidence of language ? If the elder race was in a great majority in Ionia, and even the children of the younger race learned to speak from Aegean mothers, would not the resultant vulgar speech be that of the elder race ? Yet the historic speech was, in fact, Greek, as all the world knows. The objection is reasonable ; but it does not necessarily hold good. Language is shown by experience to be changed by conquest more easily than type of civilization. Take this same land of Asia Minor at this day. What has become of Greek speech among ninety-nine hundredths of its people ? The same fate has befallen that speech which once befell its inland languages at the hands of the Greeks. The Turkish conquering minority has imposed its tongue on the aborigines of Ionia, Lydia, Phrygia, and Cappadocia alike. Yet the type of civilization and the fundamental cult-beliefs of the people are not those of the true Turks. Compare also the well-known linguistic result of the conquest of Egypt by a very small number of Arabs. Ere the migrations to Asia began, the speech of all mainland Greece may very well have already become that of the northern conquerors.

The objector's question can also be countered with another. What do we know about the language of pre-Achaean Greece ? Even if the Minoan tablets could be interpreted, they would not necessarily inform us with certainty on the point. Crete may well have had a very different tongue, as different as that remote offshoot of Indo-Germanic speech, expressed in the three uninterpreted inscriptions of Praesos, is from the language of the Gortynian Laws. The most aboriginal and conservative population of mainland Greece in the eyes of the later Hellenes was the Arcadian. Its historic dialect was very near that in which the Homeric Epics are written, and very near that of Cyprus also, which was expressed in a syllabic character, certainly a survival of the Minoan script. How do we know that this Arcadian dialect does not represent a prehistoric tongue once spoken over a large part of the Aegean area, if not in Crete ? Professor Conway, at any rate, believes this was the case. Or, again, how do we know that the common speech of later Hellas was originally that of the younger rather than of the elder element in the race ? We know, in fact, nothing of the prehistoric tongues of central Europe, nothing more than we know of the prehistoric Aegean tongues. We cannot say whether these two families were kin or not, and whether or no they differed widely Nor can we say of which tongue the later Greek dialects were a development ; or whether they were a development of

both tongues ; or, what proportion of each elder tongue
was retained. Later Greek speech may have been fundamentally mid-European, largely contaminated with Aegean
survivals ; or it may have been fundamentally Aegean with
mid-European intrusions, as our own language is fundamentally Anglo-Saxon largely contaminated by the speech
of Norman conquerors. Whatever be the facts, they are
too problematical at present for any valid argument for
or against the sub-Aegean character of Ionian civilization
to be based on linguistic grounds.

Some, who have listened to me throughout, may be
inclined to think I have made too much case of Aegean
civilization. There is a well-known tendency to find one
formula to explain all things, and an equally notorious one
to overwork the latest formula. But I submit that these
lectures are not the result of either of those tendencies.
In any case I protest that I have not been influenced by the
principle, *omne ignotum pro magnifico*. Aegean civilization
is no longer among *ignota*, as things prehistoric go. Thanks
to the richness of many of its sites and their abundant
preservation of all sorts of remains, coupled with the fact
that most of these sites remained virgin until a generation
on which scientific opinion had already imposed the obligation
to excavate in a spirit of scientific impartiality ; thanks, too,
to the not inconsiderable light thrown back by the literature
of the subsequent historic people of the area—we know
relatively more about Aegean civilization than we do about,
say, Mesopotamian. There remain many things uncertain
and many things unknown ; but there can hardly be any
aspect of its social life that has not now been illustrated,
or any general class of its products of which we have not
discovered examples. We know the latter, indeed, more
minutely and more exactly than we know the products
of the subsequent archaic Hellenic Age.

And how far does this knowledge justify a wide applica-
tion of the Aegean formula to the elucidation of the prehistoric civilization of the Nearer East ? Not only is the
dominance of this civilization over the Aegean area, during

all the prehistoric period of human productivity, back to
the neolithic age, placed beyond question by the evidence
of the deeper strata wherever they have been tapped, but
we can see that its influence ranged extraordinarily widely
outside that area, at any rate in its later period.    In the
western Mediterranean lands it has long been an accepted
fact of archaeology that prehistoric Sicily was permeated
by its latest influence—a fact which illustrates and to some
extent explains the Greek tradition that Minos and his
Cretans themselves sailed to Sicily, and that there the last
king of Aegean Crete met his death.    Hardly less conspicuous is the late Aegean influence in the cemeteries of
southern Italy, and among the antiquities even of the north-
east of the peninsula, the basin of the Po and the Venetic
province.    We find it in Sardinia, and also, according to
the latest researchers, in the prehistoric strata of southern
Spain.

In the eastern Mediterranean, Aegean culture was even
more potent, and the penetration of alien societies by its
home products more frequent.    We have yet to learn what
effect it had on the nearest coast of Africa, the Cyrenaic, and
for that reason, if no other, earnestly hope that the new era
in Turkey may soon result in the opening of this territory to
the archaeological explorer.    But about Aegean penetration
of the Nile valley there is no longer a shadow of doubt, and
continual fresh discoveries of Aegean products on Egyptian
sites show that we do not even yet know the full measure of
it.    There has been so much said on this subject since the
days when Professor Flinders Petrie found Cretan sherds
in the south-eastern Fayum among remains of the Twelfth
Dynasty, and fragments of above eight hundred Aegean
vases on the Eighteenth Dynasty site of El-Amarna, that
I need only call your attention to the further evidence
obtained by Egyptian excavators in the last two seasons.
At Abydos, where Professor Petrie had already found
evidence of commerce with Crete under the Old Empire,
Professor Garstang opened, in the spring of 1907, a tomb
of the Twelfth Dynasty which contained a perfect vase

of the peculiar and unmistakable polychrome fabric of Crete in the Middle Minoan age.  From a settlement of the same period at Rifeh, a little lower down the valley and not far from Assiut, Professor Petrie recovered about the same time other painted Aegean sherds.  The same explorer, whose eyes were the first to be opened to this class of remains in Egypt, had already obtained others from his excavations at Tell el-Yahudieh at the apex of the Delta.  More than one Aegean vase has also come lately into the hands of Cairene dealers, probably from Deltaic sites.  It is not too much to say that there is seldom any considerable excavation made nowadays in Egyptian strata of the period from the Old Empire to the Twentieth Dynasty, in which Aegean objects are not found.  Nor was there only importation of such objects.  As Professor von Bissing and Professor Naville have observed, there was local imitation of Aegean ceramics and Aegean reliefs in Egypt ; and some have long maintained that the singular naturalistic art, which marked the reign of Amenhetep IV at El-Amarna, was due to the same source whence came the enormous profusion of non-Egyptian painted vases found on the site.

To the Aegean objects found on sites in Philistia and southern Palestine I have already alluded.  At Gezer and Tell es-Safi were unearthed both Aegean and distinctively Cypriote pottery, a sword of the Aegean horned form and (as a very competent observer, Dr. Duncan Mackenzie, who visited the excavations, reports) ground-plans of buildings showing well-known Aegean features.  If Mr. Evans gains acceptance for his theory that the linear characters, incised on sherds found at Tell el-Hesy, are derived from the Minoan linear script, and that, directly or indirectly, both the north and the south Semitic systems owned the same parentage, the evidence of Aegean penetration will be stronger still.  About Aegean influence on Phoenicia I have spoken likewise.  Long ago Monsieur Heuzey of the Louvre pointed out the obvious relation between certain terra-cottas, found on the Lebanon littoral, and a well-known Cypriote class, Since we now know that the latter class derived its character not from Phoenician originals but from the indigenous sub-Aegean art of the island itself, these Phoenician terra-cottas are good evidence of that Aegean influence which is reasonably to be looked for on the Asiatic mainland in the near neighbourhood of so productive a centre of Aegean art as Cyprus.

Finally, omitting Asia Minor, whose case, being the one *sub iudice*, would involve the argument in a vicious circle, let me remind you of that large continental area in south-eastern Europe, which produces such abundant remains of a culture closely akin to the Aegean. This area radiated influence in its turn to the far north and west, to inspire the beautiful ornamentation of prehistoric Scandinavia and of Keltic art in Ireland and Great Britain. A full knowledge and a right understanding 'of Danubian and Balkan antiquities are of peculiar importance to the problem under discussion. The evidence indicates that we have to do not with a culture derived from the Aegean, but with a local independent development, which proceeded along lines closely parallel to the course of the latter. If we cannot yet venture to say certainly that the Danubian and Aegean peoples were kin, we can see clearly that their cultures were so closely related that, in a rough and large classification, they might well be grouped together as one. The whole of south-eastern Europe and the Isles might be marked as the common area of an Aegeo-Danubian civilization.

The Aegean culture, which had occupied thus completely the later Hellenic area, enveloping it with influences radiating to points more distant than the Hellenic would reach again for many centuries, would have had to be reckoned with first and foremost in the problem of the origins of Greek civilization, even had it attained to a far less high stage of culture than its remains compel us to credit. These, however, speak to a degree of social achievement which must have left, in the area of its prevalence, a mark as deep and ineffaceable as those left by the Nilotic and Meso-potamian civilizations. If this seems to you too strong a statement, consider for one moment both the spirit and the execution of the best products of Aegean art that have been recovered. Take as examples, among many, the ivory figurines and faience reliefs of Cnossus, or the carved steatite vases of Hagia Triada; the polychrome egg-shell pottery of the 'Kamáres' class, or the goldsmiths' work on the Vaphio cups and the Mycenae dagger-blades; the gem-cutters' work on the finest intaglios, or the painted scenes on the great sarcophagus from Hagia Triada. You have to go to the 'Sheikh el-beled' statue at Cairo, if you would find a parallel to the naturalistic execution of the tiny Cnossian ivories : to the best animal sculptures of the Eighteenth Pharaonic dynasty, and the supreme moment of Assyrian art, as illustrated by the lion-hunt of Assur-banipal, or by the enamelled reliefs of Shalmaneser the Second's time at Assur, if you are seeking worthy comparisons with the Cnossian plaque which shows a wild nanny-goat suckling her kid. But when you pass on to the Hagia Triada cups, and the Kamáres pottery, you find yourself at a loss. There is no such naturalistic treatment of the human form in relief among the remains of either Egyptian or Mesopotamian art, not even at El-Amarna ; and there is no ceramic fabric of any ancient Oriental civilization really comparable to the best 'Kamáres' ware. Nor again have we outside the Aegean any such examples of pictorial inlay work in gold alloys, as that lavished on the Mycenae blades. It is especially significant, that whenever a critic has essayed comment on the Aegean artist's effort to realize the ideal by close study of nature—such an effort as that which transformed foreign models on the gaming-casket of Enkomi, or in the lotus decoration on a Cretan vase from Zakro— he has invariably had to come far down the ages to find something worthy to be compared. The finest period of later Hellenic art, not any period of Oriental art, has always seemed to offer the earliest standard of comparison.

Or, leaving the fine arts, without mention of a tithe of the various techniques, look to the Aegean mastery of more practical things. Consider the sanitary and hydraulic

appliances of the Cnossian palace, or the structural skill
which could pile story above story and fashion the broad
stairways flight after flight. Consider the arithmetical
knowledge of fractional and proportional values clearly
attested by the entries on the Cnossian tally-tablets. Take
account of the evidence of a highly civilized and sumptuous
social life which must be inferred from the wealth of decoration lavished on all sorts of furniture, great and small, from
the elaborate dress of women, from the representations of
sports and scenes of festivity, from the importation of the
products of distant civilizations. I need not labour the
argument. You cannot pass an hour in the museum of
Candia, or the Mycenae room at Athens, without feeling
that you are in presence of products of a civilization whose
tradition would have died very hard, even had it been
attacked by men utterly barbarian. But barbarian, as I
have already suggested, those who did attack it were in all
probability far from being. To substantiate this statement
let me dwell for a few minutes, ere concluding, on the mid-
European antiquities which are probably not very familiar
to you, having been published in part in somewhat in-
accessible treatises.

Those which concern our problem consist in pottery,
weapons, terra-cotta figurines and other objects of the late
Neolithic, Bronze, and earliest Iron Ages. For it was in
the last of these periods that we must suppose the chief
southward migrations to have taken place, if, as is universally
assumed, the Aegean societies were overcome by the
northerners' use of iron weapons. Certainly Homer's
Achaeans, whom we regard as the first main wave of migrants,
are represented as knowing iron, though the use of bronze
was still common ; and in certain Cretan and Attic tombs,
dated by their pottery to the last centuries of the second
millennium B.C., the two metals have been found together.
If this view be correct, as there is every reason to think, all
the evidence found on the Neolithic, Bronze Age, and
earliest Iron Age sites in the Danube basin has to be
taken into account when we are dealing with the northern

migrants who descended on Greece at the end of the Aegean Age.

These sites lie across virtually the whole continental space from the northern shore of the Black Sea to the eastern Alps. No migratory people could have entered the Balkan Peninsula during the periods stated without coming into some contact with the culture to which these sites bear witness. Their northern boundary, so far as known at present, runs from Kieff in Russia to the Attersee in south-western Austria, and the areas in which similar sites have been found include Bessarabia, Roumania, Servia, and Bosnia. Nor is this all. A series of similar sites comes south through Thrace into north-western Asia Minor and through Macedonia into Thessaly. The First City at Hissarlik and the cemetery of Yortan in Mysia appear to belong to the group ; so do the earliest remains on several Thessalian sites, e. g. Dimini, Sesklo, and the hillock of Zerelia lately explored by two members of the British School at Athens, Messrs. Wace and Droop.

On almost all these sites the earliest human products are neolithic, and show such local varieties of form and ornament that they must be regarded as, in the main, of local manufacture. That is to say, there was production taking place at scores of places all over south-eastern Europe at a very remote date, long before that of the Hellenic migrations. Nor was it by any means only the rudest sort of production. At Butmir in Bosnia, in a cemetery where no metal occurred, were found vases with both moulded and incised returning-spiral decoration, which is as finely drawn and artistically disposed as any of the simpler spiral ornamentation known anywhere : also fragments of clay figurines showing considerable skill in modelling the human form, and very fine chipped flints and polished stone weapons. Nor are spirals the only ornament. There is great variety of geometric patterns, often picked out in white by powdered filling. Clay idols found under similar circumstances at Cucuteni in Roumania show a most elaborate decoration of lines following the contours of the figure and producing the effect of tattooed skin. But the crown of Danubian neolithic decoration is represented by the Bessarabian pottery found at Petrény by Dr. von Stern, with its beautiful violet pigment on reddish-brown ground, its beginnings of polychromy, and its not ill-drawn representations of animal forms and even the human figure.

Some have maintained that this Danubian neolithic work is much later than Aegean decorated neolithic ; but the best authority, Dr. Hoernes, holds the former to be even the earlier. It may be pointed out that the stratification of the Hissarlik mound, where the lowest layer of sub-neolithic time contains ware closely akin to the Danubian, and whorls incised with symbols remarkably like those noticed at Tordos in Transylvania, tells very strongly in favour of the Danubian neolithic period having been about as early in time as the Aegean. In any case it will hardly be maintained by any serious archaeologist that it was not long anterior to the supposed date of the southward Hellenic migration. And if no more than that be conceded, it is still amply sufficient for our present purpose.

With the appearance of bronze there is evidence of rapid advance in fabric and decoration, as the fine clay cups of Lengyel in Hungary, the weapons, vessels, and toilet objects in bronze of Glasinatz in Bosnia, and the terra-cottas of Klitzevatz in Servia, are enough to prove, even without the remarkable contents of the earlier graves opened at Hallstatt in the Salzkammergut on the western frontier of the Danubian area. And analogies to Bronze Age products of the Aegean become so frequent and close that it is difficult not to infer some intercourse and communication of influences between the two civilizations, even if there had been none in neolithic times. Some authorities, indeed, e. g. von Stern, think even that the neolithic art of the Aegean was derived from inner Europe, through some migratory movement. But the curious fact that neolithic products are rudest in Crete, and progress in excellence up through Melos and the Cyclades to the Balkans, favours rather the reversal of this derivation. In any case, however, independent origins in art so primitive as the neolithic are the more probable. The interesting series of parallel Bronze Age forms and decorative motives, set out by Reinhold Freiherr von Lichtenburg in his *Beiträge zur ältesten Geschichte von Kypros* in the Proceedings of the Berliner Vorderasiatische Gesellschaft for 1906, ought to be consulted by every one interested in the problem of Hellenic origins.

The transition to the Iron Age is best attested by the great mass of the Hallstatt objects, among which are many which remind us of the earliest known Hellenic bronzes, as well as of the earliest known Italian. The highest art of the latter is represented by the magnificent *situlae* of the Villanova type, first found near Bologna, in which we seem to see the meeting of two artistic influences of south and north, as in the steatite vases of Hagia Triada in Crete. That the movement of culture was rather to southward from the Danubian area, than to northward from the Mediterranean, there can be little doubt. The general direction of migrations, the long evolution of culture in the Danubian basin, and the comparative eclipse of Mediterranean art in the period immediately preceding the archaic Hellenic age, all support the theory of southward movement having been responsible for such analogies as are observed in Aegean and Danubian products. It is noteworthy that a similar eclipse seems to have occurred in the Danubian area soon after the local invention or adoption of iron. In some districts, especially those near the Black Sea, the eclipse began even earlier. The natural inference is that for a very long time barbarous peoples had been constantly pressing down from the vast Russian country upon the Danubian area, and that finally they more or less completely submerged its civilization.

Such pressure would account for those secondary southward movements of Balkan peoples which resulted in the Achaean, Dorian, and Ionian invasions of the Greek and Anatolian peninsulas. These, composed of refugee elements long domiciled in the area of Danubian culture, brought with them its products and traditions to inspire new life into the flagging Aegean world. Though worsted in the struggle with the northernmost Europeans, we may reasonably suppose the invaders still to have been more vigorous and less developed than the southern peoples. It is the opinion of many authorities, but it cannot yet be proved by anthropological evidence, that the Danubian peoples were themselves drawn in a large measure from the same great human family to which the Aegean societies owed their fundamental stock. This was the small dark Mediterranean Race, which seems to have been the most artistic of early mankind. This may be allowed to be a probable opinion, if large allowance be made for the contamination which age-long residence on the frontiers of another family must have entailed : for, certainly, the coloration of the Achaeans, as Homer describes them, points to some other and more northerly element in the earliest of the Hellenic migrations. In any case, however, it is absurd to suppose that any of the prehistoric societies of this debated region of the Nearer East, so desirable in the eyes of the populations of the deserts, steppes, and forests of three continents, were still unmixed even in neolithic time. So far back as the anthropologist has been able to obtain evidence in Crete alone, he has found himself confronted by varieties of physical structure, which, whatever classification he adopts, forbid him to argue purity of race.

Such was the culture of the Danubian and Balkan area. However it originated—and the evidence of neolithic settlements points strongly to spontaneous origin in the Aegean and Danubian areas respectively, and to subsequent developments on parallel lines, conditioned by racial kinship, and modified perhaps by intercourse—it must have exercised a compelling effect on the migrants, who passed through its province, even if they did not spring from that province. And it had been there for ages before their final descent into the Aegean area.

I alluded at the opening of this course to a feeling, still entertained by a few fervent Hellenists, especially in this country and in Germany, that it savours of profanity to affiliate the Hellenic to other civilizations—to give it, in fact, an earthly pedigree. That feeling deserves no consideration; for nothing is more genuinely Hellenic than to try to make phenomena intelligible. The supposed phenomenon of a savage horde, which had been moving westwards for long ages through central Asian deserts and Russian steppes, suddenly and spontaneously developing art so soon as it came into a certain stimulating natural environment, and incontinently soaring to the highest artistic expression which the world has seen, is not intelligible, but among things miraculous. Progress is not so made *per saltum* even by a Chosen Race. But traced back on the one side to the immemorial culture of the Aegean, on the other to the vigorous culture of mid-Europe, the development of Greek civilization can be presented with all the depth of true perspective. We are not denying to the Hellenes anything that they made their own by detecting a premonition of their artistic spirit in the sculptures and paintings of prehistoric Crete. Nor shall we belittle their place in the story of human progress, if we suggest that their social and political ideals originated in that continental area, whose later tribal and communal organizations so greatly impressed the Romans when they first came to know the Germanic peoples.

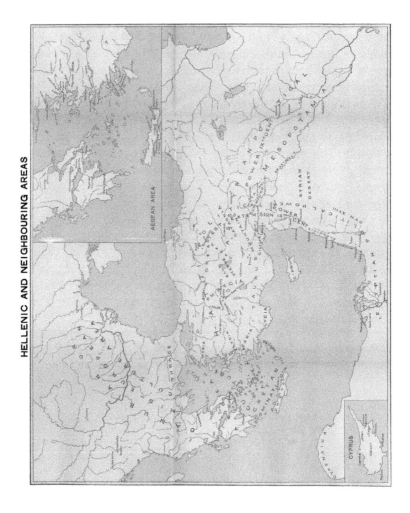

HELLENIC AND NEIGHBOURING AREAS

The material originally positioned here is too large for reproduction in this reissue. A PDF can be downloaded from the web address given on page iv of this book, by clicking on 'Resources Available'.

www.ingramcontent.com/pod-product-compliance
Ingram Content Group UK Ltd.
Pitfield, Milton Keynes, MK11 3LW, UK
UKHW042151280225
455719UK00001B/258